SpiritArts

Transformation through Creating Art, Music and Dance

by Lynn Miller

Published by Expressive Therapy Press
125 Prospect St.
Phoenixville, PA 19460

Note to the Reader:
The exercises in this book are given as information to expand your knowledge but are not to be a substitute for medical or psychological treatment with a professional when needed.

SpirtArts:
Transformation through Creating Art, Music and Dance

ISBN: 978-0-615-84150-2

Cover design and book layout by Jill Carter

Endorsements

I have read many books about the arts and spirituality over my lifetime and I am astonished by Lynn Miller's ***SpiritArts!*** It may be one of the most important summations of the world's present ways of becoming aware and involved with the "Artist" that we are born as.

I have known this renaissance person for many years and have always been inspired and impressed by her genius talents in dance, painting, sculpture, music, art, creative arts therapy and healing.

SpiritArts, *is simply the best and most informative text on the "Arts" that I am aware of. Lynn's style of writing is inviting, friendly and easy to understand, as if you were listening to one telling the 'Truth'. Her humanism is clear and her research is impressive.*

The personal stories of her experiences also give us a feeling of the common touch and helps readers become informed about the miracle that we are all born as gifted creative humans and that we are meant to be our unique expressive self. There is nobody like us!!! We are each unique!!!

We humans need to express ourselves daily through our chosen Art and with kindness toward all of life. I highly recommend this superb book. Lynn has written perhaps the seminal book of our time in the allied arts and what they mean.

- David Darling
Grammy Award winning cellist,
composer and teacher

SpiritArts *is a must for every expressive therapist. Lynn Miller uses many of the expressive arts she explored through her own journey of growth and joyfully and passionately shares the many wonderful ideas for all of us to use. Included are many sensory exercises helping us find our inner wisdom connecting us back to our inspired, creative source.*

- Teresa Benzwie, Ed.D., L.C.S.W. Is a psychotherapist in private practice and author of ***A Moving Experience*** and **Numbers on the Move.** She trains Temple University students in using the arts to teach all areas of the early classroom curriculum.

"In ***SpiritArts****, Lynn Miller gifts us with a rich and diverse tool box for unlocking our joy, creativity, and wonder. Thank you, Lynn, for this generous work and your generous heart. "*

- Elizabeth Frediani, author of ***Where Body Meets Soul: Subtle Energy Healing Practices for Physical and Spiritual Self-Care.***

Table of Contents

Endorsements i

Foreward 1

Prelude 2

Introduction 4

How to Use this Book 6

Materials You Will Need 7

How You Can Benefit from SpiritArts 8

Section 1: The Method 11

Creativity, Improvisation and Spirit 12

SpiritArts 4-Step Process 14

Step 1: The Breath 15

Step 2: Body Awareness 18

Step 3: Connect with the Heart 20

Step 4: Deep Listening 22

Spirit of Improvisation 24

Obstacles: Facing Fears 25

Cultivating Awareness 27

Facing the Unknown 28

Surrender: Let the Materials Guide You 32

Love Your Art, Your Art Loves You 34

Spirituality and the Creative Process 36

Nine Cycles of the Creative Process 40

Manifestation through Transformation 43

Section 2: Let's Create 53

Inner Dance 58

Spirit of Music Improvisation 63

Exploring the Voice 66

Spirit of Musical Instruments 73

Exploring Scales 83

Exploring Free Improvisation 85

Spirit of Visual Art 86

Drawing on the Outer World 87

Drawing on the Inner World 90

Spirit Painting 91

Exploring Materials 93

How Music, Dance and Visual Art are Connected 95

Section 3: Arts and Healing 101

Archetypes 103

The Shadow 104

Expressing Feelings 106

Self-witnessing 110

Processing Imagery Through Combining Art Forms 117

Healing Vibrationally 126

Toning 128

Balancing the Chakras with Sound and Color 135

SpiritArts and Life Integration 143

It Takes a Village to Write a Book 148

About the Artist 148

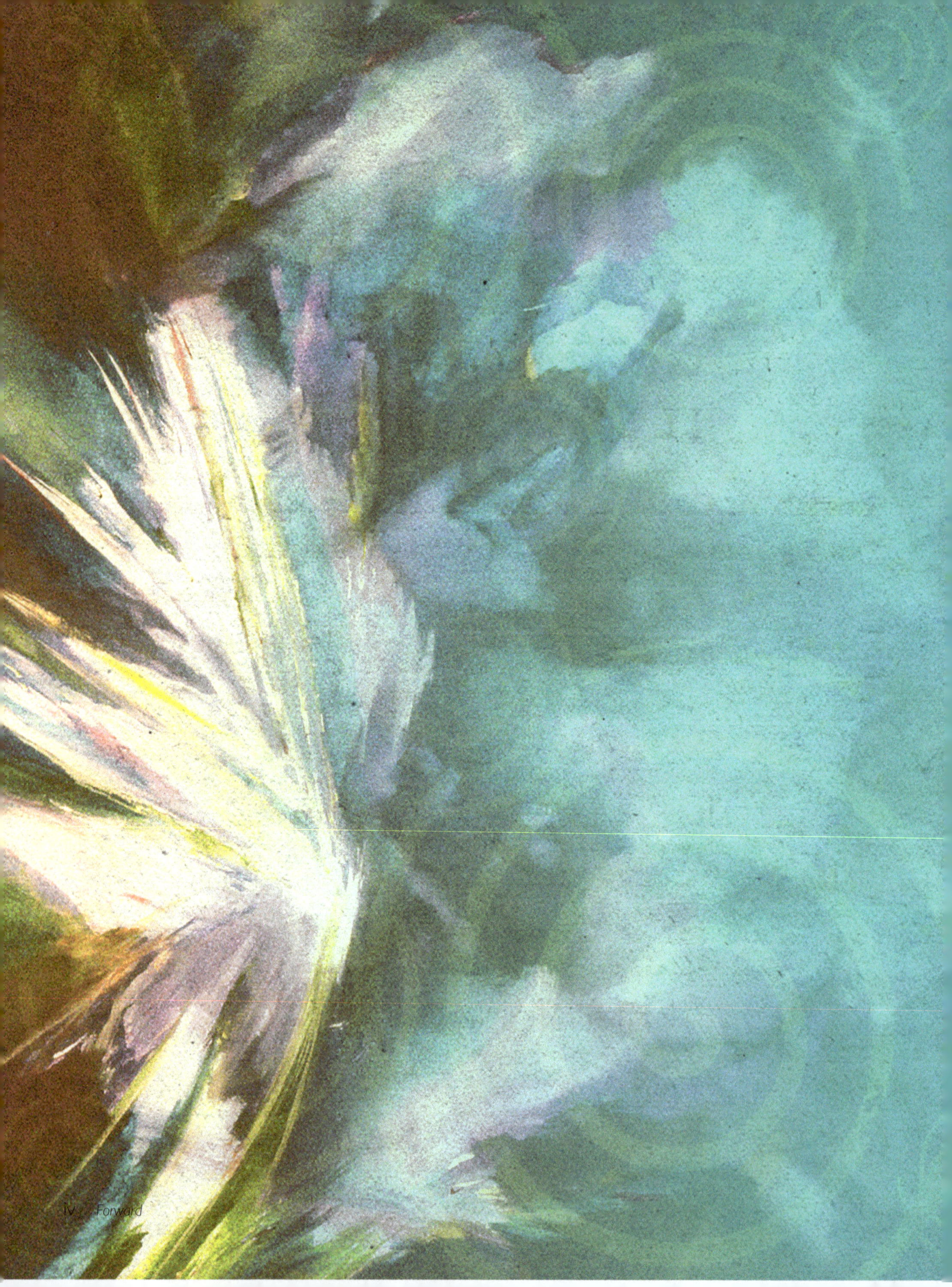

Foreward

Lynn Miller is one of the most creative multimedia artists that I have ever known. Not only does she produce exciting works of her own, but she also inspires people in her community to reach out and explore their own creative gifts.

I first met Lynn when she invited me to her hometown of Phoenixville, PA, to teach my Vibrational Healing workshops, where I had the opportunity to witness firsthand the effects of her life upon that community. I lived there for two weeks, and little by little Lynn's story unfolded.

Back in 1993 Ms. Miller arrived in Phoenixville, a former iron and steel town outside of Philadelphia. With the steel industry leaving in the 80's, it was practically a ghost town. Historically, in 1813 the supervisor of the mill actually had a ***bona fide*** vision of the Phoenix coming out of the foundry fires. He saw the mythical Phoenix bird dying and being reborn from the flames. The vision inspired him to rename the factory ***Phoenix Works*** and the town changed its name to Phoenixville.

Lynn realized there was something special about this town with the Phoenix as its namesake. Inspired by the theme of the burning Phoenix, Ms. Miller had a vision to make a mosaic mural with the community with the Phoenix image. After the mural was complete, of course they had to have a full costume parade to celebrate. She invited the community to make giant 20' puppets with her for the parade.

Years later she coordinated artists to help build a huge wooden Phoenix sculpture and set it on fire for a Firebird Festival. The burning ritual was repeated as a yearly event—under the watchful supervision of the local fire department—and each year the bird got bigger and the audience doubled and tripled and quadrupled until Phoenixville became known as a hip place to live. Formerly boarded-up buildings were renovated stylishly into restaurants, coffee houses with open mikes and cute boutiques. Phoenixville became a mecca of creativity, and the weekends would find musicians, jugglers and mimes on every street corner.

So much of this was inspired at least in part by Lynn Miller. So no one is better equipped to inspire you with a vast number of exercises and activities, to enhance your own creativity. We are fortunate that Lynn has produced this book, which can greatly enrich your life. It is a manual for developing your creative self and transforming your life through the arts, much like the Phoenix.

- Joy Gardner, Author of ***Vibrational Healing through the Chakras with Light, Color, Sound, Crystals and Aromatherapy***

Prelude

Many years ago, I intuitively heard an inner message: "You are to write a book." I thought to myself, "Who, me? That's impossible!" Throughout most of my life, I had difficulty articulating my thoughts. I was unsure and had a fear of saying the wrong thing. I felt it was safer to withhold my words. Therefore, I had experienced much of my life on a nonverbal plane. Looking, listening, afraid to speak up and to say what I really felt, I had adapted by expressing myself through the arts. Because words had never come easily to me, I realized that completing this book would truly be my rite of passage. This book is about opening to possibilities.

During the summer of 2004, I had a dream while I was teaching for ***Music for People*** at the Kientalerhof – a retreat center in Switzerland. The dream said that I was to start a training course in the arts. I did not necessarily wake up ecstatic with this idea: "What a lot of work. Work that probably will involve more writing!" Additionally, I was going through an intense internal struggle involving my personal power.

The next morning, I met with Marlise Binetti, who would become my dearest friend. This long, tall Texan was a dancer and artist who had lived in Switzerland for many years. We quickly decided to develop a course together; my passion for the task began to soar. Marlise asked so many questions that answering them all required me to articulate my own ideas, which I recorded in our idea journal. That was the beginning of the book you are now reading.

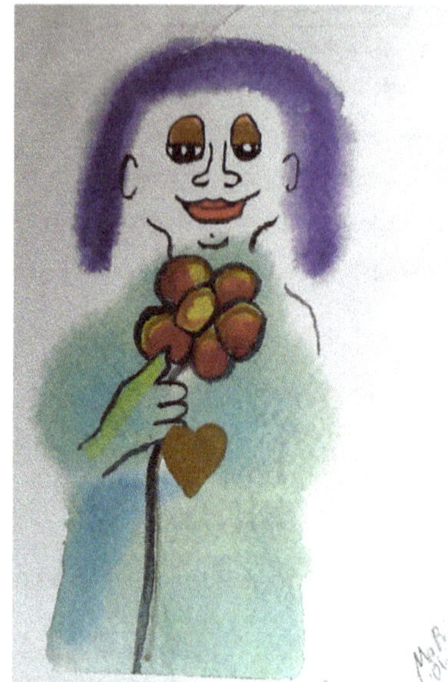

Painting by Marlise Binetti, June, 2006

Marlise died of cancer in 2006. When I returned to my idea journal, there was a handwritten note from my friend: "Lynn, Thanx for keeping notes and… for the flow, inspiration, enthusiasm, push, questions, Juice!! We are exactly at the right place…and on our way." I dedicate this book to Marlise for her inspiration and guidance – and, yes, we are on our way.

When you allow your life to be guided by spirit, you open yourself to dreams larger than your own. At one time in my life, I had little self confidence to pursue my dreams. I had no idea how to translate my passion of the arts into the world, into a career, or even where I would find my niche. I was told like many others that you cannot make a living in the arts.

However, if you listen and are willing to take a risk, (and are willing to risk the journey) the answers will come. In my case, I was standing in the kitchen one day with the sunlight shining on my head like a light bulb. I realized that I really liked working with people and that I wanted to use music and the arts for healing (although I had no clue what that meant). Fortunately, someone told me about music therapy. Shortly thereafter, I synchronistically met a music therapist, Eric Miller, who is now my husband. I, too, became a music therapist and am forever grateful to have found a path that incorporates both my work and my passion!

Years later, I discovered Expressive Arts Therapy. I felt right at home in a profession that therapeutically incorporates all the arts. I feel gifted to be influenced by Natalie Rogers, Shaun McNiff, and Aviva Gold – my mentors in the Expressive Arts Therapy field. I am equally grateful for the experience that Eric and I had in creating a nonprofit organization, ***Expressive Therapy Concepts*** (ExpressiveTherapy.org), with the intention of bringing the healing arts to our communities. In the '90's, we put on several ***Expressive Arts Therapies*** and ***Integrative Medicine*** conferences, gifting us with the opportunity to be in the company of many leaders in these fields.

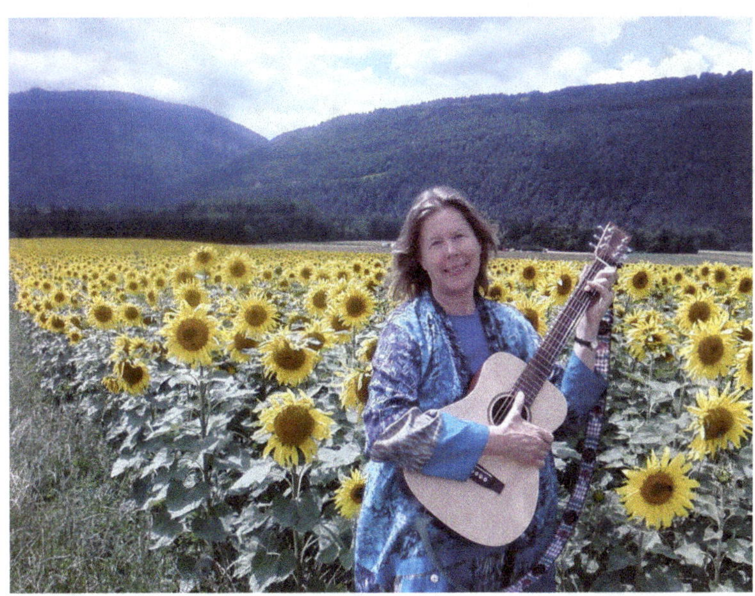

Lynn Miller, Switzerland

Music for People (musicforpeople.org), founded by David Darling and Bonnie Insull, has been another transformative influence in my life. ***Music for People*** (MfP) holds the philosophy that music is for everyone. MfP's four-year training program in music improvisation attracts both highly trained and novice musicians wanting to learn musical and leadership skills. When I began the program, I would never have guessed that I would become the Musicianship Facilitator, and my husband Eric, the Executive Director.

Elizabeth Frediani, author of ***Where Body Meets Soul***, has been my guide in physical and spiritual self-care through subtle energy. I was trained in her wonderful work, ***Chakra Clearing with Applied Integration***. Many of her practices have influenced several of the energy exercises in this book. As I claim my place as an energy healer, my life and work have expanded beyond my dreams.

I am also grateful for being in the company of Joy Gardner, author of 11 healing books, including ***Vibrational Healing***. She opened me to the world of vibrational healing and helped me claim my place as a sound healer.

Now, when I close my eyes, I can see myself back on a sunflower farm in Switzerland. The sunflowers slowly move their heads to face the sun. They look like fields of happy people. The high winds make everything come alive with breath, motion and sound. The Swiss chard dances in the fields and the telephone poles whistle at night. I can hear the wind blowing in my ears. The leaves talk, the wheat whispers and the water laughs. All these sounds of nature focus my attention and remind me how everything is connected – me, the sunflowers and you. We are all together on this mystery tour of life. The tree stands still to teach us how to move with the wind by being grounded. We give back to the tree by acknowledging its beauty. We are blessed with being able to move, to make a sound, to have a thought and to act on it – to create!

Introduction

Do you have an inner desire to express yourself creatively? Is your soul calling you to sing, dance, draw, create music? ***SpiritArts*** is not only for trained or experienced artists, but also for undiscovered ones – who know in their souls that they need to create but do not know where to begin. It is for all who want to build a relationship with their intuitive voice and inner spirit, and who desire creative expression in their life.

What skills do you need? The most important skill in the creative process is to show up. You may want to create art, dance or make music in your deepest heart; yet find you are distracted away from your very desire. ***SpiritArts*** is a guide back to self through the creative process, connecting heart with body and soul.

In the beginning...

Your creativity is your birthright. Most of us entered this world with wonder – an enchantment with what we saw, heard and felt. In our beginning on this planet, while still ***in utero***, we connected with the outer world through sound. At birth, our first connection to the world was through our breath, or a sound that we made following an exploration of our body in this new space.

None of us came here with language. That was learned. Universally, babies make similar sounds no matter their nationality. Most of us arrived with the ability to make sounds of all languages. Before language, we thought in images – our earliest language. As children, many of us explored freely with images, stories, movement and song.

Where did this creative impulse come from? When did it slow down and why? How can we reconnect with it? ***SpiritArts*** is here to give you support on taking the steps to reclaim your creative self.

My beginning...

Because the arts were always a refuge for me – a safe place – I never outgrew that creative impulse from childhood. The rest of the world didn't always feel safe to me. I didn't know where I fit in. So, in many ways, I checked out.

My first medium of expressing myself creatively was through dance. I remember putting on performances for my parents with a frilly slip over my head. I spent a lot of the day with the slip on my head: it was a veil and I was the bride. My mother was a Southern belle, a symbol of femininity. My father was domineering, macho and controlling, a symbol of masculinity (in the old school of being male or female.)

When I was growing up, it was not attractive for a woman to do anything better than her male counterpart. Women downplayed their attributes. So I played dumb; this was one of the ways I gave up my power. I was taught to sit up and shut up. In our patriarchal household, a child's opinion was not valued – especially a female child's. In our familial relationships, I suppressed my opinions and my voice, beginning my journey of expressing myself through non-verbal arts.

Going through school, I began to further disconnect. I did not feel good enough. Art was not particularly respected unless you were a performer, in a gallery or played in a certain style. I loved my art, but I did not know how to bring it into the world. This work has culminated from my own healing of reclaiming my power and true self through the arts.

Once I connected with myself, I was able to connect with others. I feel that bringing the arts back to the people is important for humankind. I have personally worked with people of all ages, different cultures, backgrounds and abilities through the arts. I have used the arts for community building, team building, creating community rituals, festivals and parades, as well as working therapeutically, teaching and performing. Through improvisation, I have learned to live my life more fully, openly and joyfully. I would like to share all of this with you, to help you remember your own creative self.

How to Use this Book

The exercises throughout the book vary from energetic meditations to art techniques and processes. It is essential that you experience them; otherwise, it will only be an intellectual exercise for you. Spend time with the exercises. The only way to really understand the material is through experiencing it.

SpiritArts is organized into three sections:

- Section I - THE METHOD states the philosophy, methods, and principles. It addresses creative blocks and provides exercises to work with them.

- Section II - LET'S CREATE contains structures and exercises for approaching each art form from within, and for broadening your artistic expression. The forms are designed for both beginners and for those with more experience. If you are having any difficulty working with these exercises, refer back to Section I. If some of the arts exercises seem too advanced for you, consider that particular exercise to be written for more experienced readers. Skip it and focus on the exercises more suitable for your level of experience.

- Section III - ARTS AND HEALING provides structures for deepening your creative experience, and helping you to be a clearer creative channel. This section provides skills in healing self and others through emotional processing through the arts. Skills will also be introduced in vibrational healing through sound, color and energy.

Materials You Will Need

SpiritArts provides experiences in visual art, music and dance. Even if you do not have experience in any of these art modalities, I encourage you to pick up a paintbrush, sing and dance. Trying all of the art forms will deepen your process. Have these materials on hand for the exercises:

- **Journal:** Keep a journal documenting your thoughts, feelings and observations using color, symbols or words. Create a free-form account of your inner experiences: your desires, breakthroughs, ecstasies. The journal will become a container for intimate contact with yourself.

  Another option is to create a ***visual journal*** with drawings and collections of images that catch your interest, such as cards and other printed materials. Or, you may prefer a ***sonic journal*** for recording your musical creations and developing a playlist of music that is interesting to you.

- **Comfortable Clothes:** When doing movement exercises, be sure to wear comfortable, loose fitting clothes.

For **visual art** you will need:

- **Oil Pastels:** They are economical, brilliant in color, and easy to use. Water-soluble oil pastels (such as the ones manufactured by ***Portfolio***) offer even more versatility. You can use them to create transparent as well as solid opaque colors, depending on how much water you add with the brush.
- **Water-based Paints:** These can be watercolor tubes, acrylics, or tempura. Begin with the basic colors of red, yellow, blue, black, and white. They come in many hues; pick the ones you like. You can then mix other colors with these primary colors or buy your favorites.
- **Paintbrushes:** Get lots of sizes and shapes, large to small. Sponges are great. You can even use your hands.
- **Multimedia materials:** Magazines, tissue paper, glue, scissors, felt, glitter.
- **Paper/Posterboard:** Posterboard can be cut into smaller pieces or you can use a heavyweight paper such as ***Bristol.*** The heavyweight papers will hold the water. If you are working with watercolors, you may choose watercolor paper.
- **Clay:** Sculpey, children's modeling clay or self-hardening pottery clay.

For **music** you will need:

- **Your Voice:** It's free.
- **Drum:** A frame drum, djembe, or thick plastic bucket.
- **Instrument:** Do you have an instrument that you play or that has been sitting in the corner waiting to be played? Pull it out. It has been waiting for you.
- **Want a new instrument?** Try a Native American flute, dulcimer, ukulele, kalimba, rainstick, or shakers. All of these instruments are accessible with a little guidance.
- **Inspiring recorded music**
- **Claim a place** either in your house or elsewhere, where you can create. Make it a safe place to go within yourself.

How You Can Benefit from SpiritArts

The intention of this book is to help you develop a spiritual practice through art making and to develop art making through a spiritual path. ***SpiritArts*** is nourishment for the soul, leading you toward the path of who you really are. Our creations are a direct connection to the source; this connection opens doors to our inner voice, developing intuition.

The exercises begin simply, yet profoundly. I believe we are capable of creating music, art, and dance without years of education. Technique that is taught in school is helpful but not necessary for creative expression.

As children, many of us jumped effortlessly from one art form to another. Some of us sang, danced, painted, acted, and had imaginary friends whom we would now call spirit guides. Some people find they are more comfortable in one art form than another. This insight tells us how we take in the world as well as what kind of learners we are.

SpiritArts is a body-centered approach to the arts and spirit. There is a spiritual philosophy that everything we know is within. We will approach each art form from the inside out through our bodies. Our bodies have innate wisdom that our thinking mind does not always understand or listen to. The energetic meditations and exercises throughout the book help us tune in to our inner landscapes, emotions and the rich imagery within our imagination.

This book provides concrete suggestions about how to connect with creative spirit. You will learn how to create from within, authentically. This is helpful whether you are a beginner or an experienced artist, musician, writer, or dancer. Philosophically, we all have creative potential; some simply have more experience.

Exercises in several art modalities will be presented, along with instructions on how they can integrate with each other. Painting has a lot in common with music, such as composition and listening for the end to determine when it is finished. Music has similarities to visual art, such as texture and rhythm. Movement mirrors painting with contrast, shapes, and form.

Improvisational techniques will be explored in all of the art forms. To improvise is to create in the moment. Through improvisation, we develop skills in deep listening – listening to our inner wisdom, listening to one another, listening to ourselves and trusting our impulses. Improvisation does not need to be difficult or complicated. Whenever we speak, we are improvising and creating in the moment.

As you journey through the processes in this book, you will encounter and address blocks, resistance, and all the "monkeys of the mind" that have kept you from becoming the creative being you are. As you claim your creative self, you will become self-empowered. As you develop self-confidence, you will seek to create with others, creating community.

Skills in art-making, musicianship, and movement will develop your inner artist, musician, and/or dancer. If you are a teacher, therapist, or facilitator, many of the exercises developed for going deeper into artistry can be used with groups. The cooperative exercises can also be used for team building in school and work environments.

The same process used to create music, art, and movement in the moment can also be applied for the purpose of healing. The healing power of the arts will be explored through color, sound, and body awareness. The body has a wisdom that, if listened to, is a healing guide. Creating and working with our images provides a guide to work through emotions and clear the psyche. Vibrational healing through color, sound, and energy can heal the body – even the planet!

If you are interested in transforming your life, ***SpiritArts*** is a guide encompassing art, body, heart, and spirit as your teacher. My intention for this guide is to introduce more joy into your life.

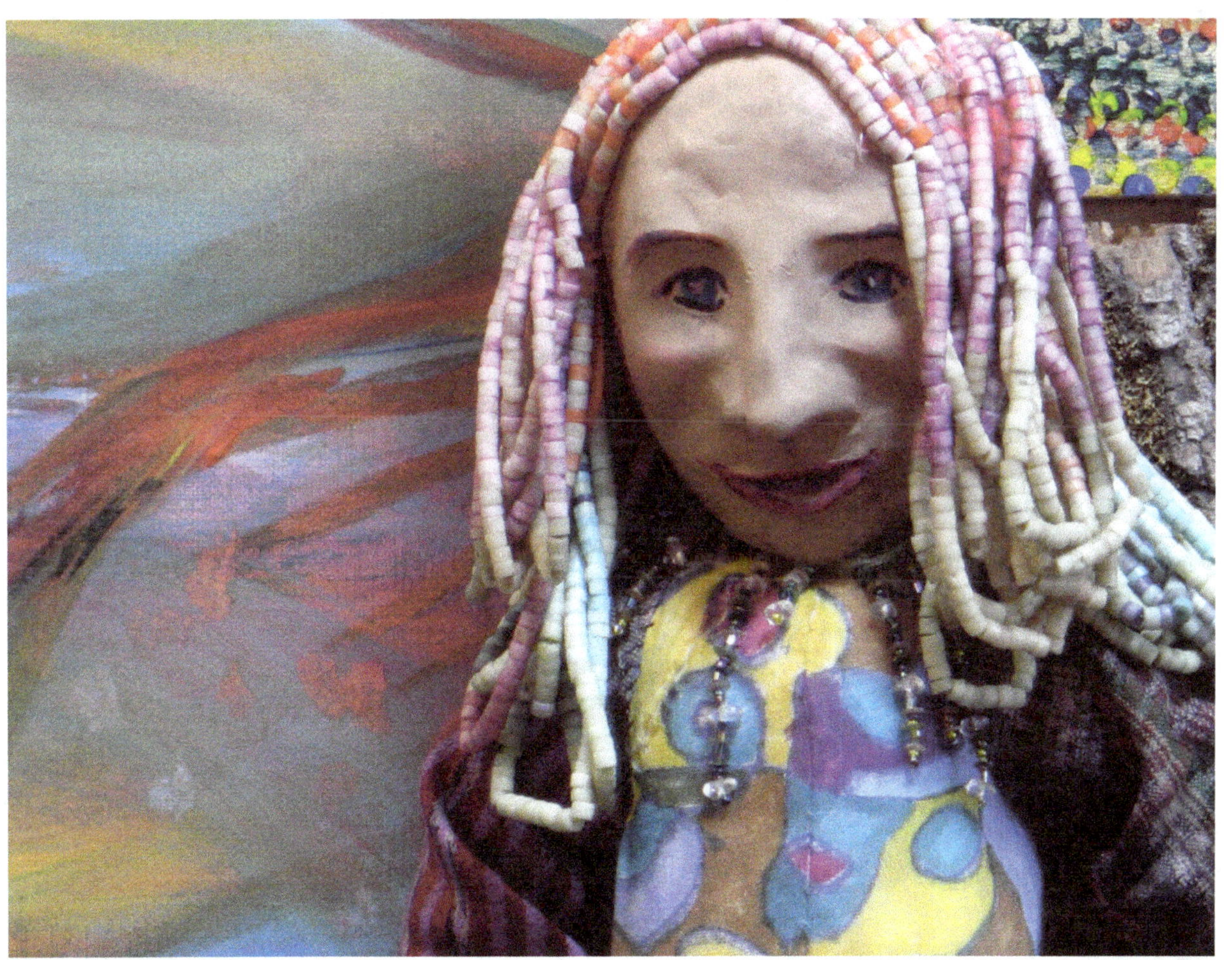

Doll by Lynn Miller

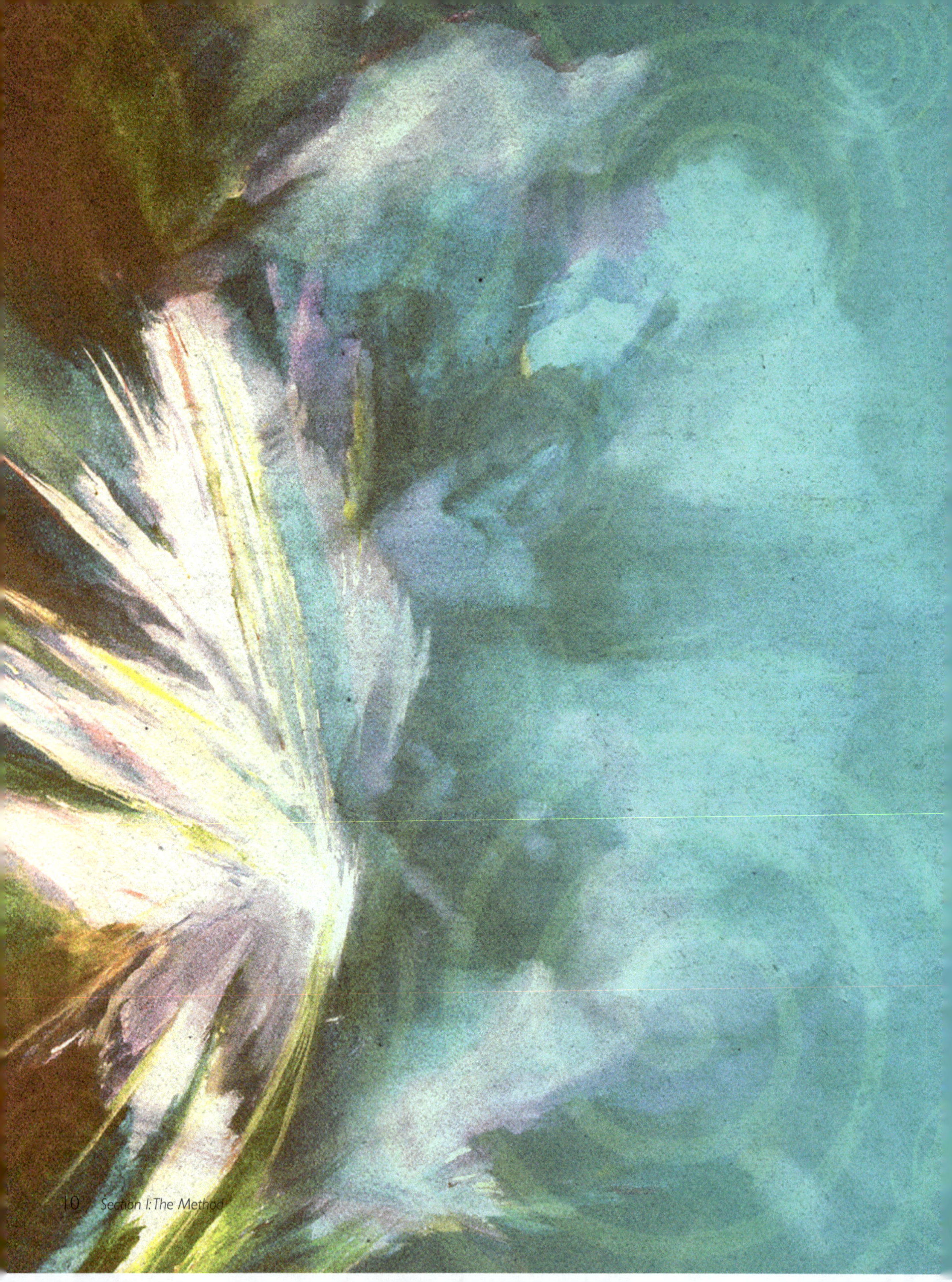

Section 1: The Method

The first section of SpiritArts provides the theories of creating art authentically, whether it be visual art, music, or dance. Come back to these methods when you find yourself blocked or needing a way to begin.

Discover the common threads between spirituality and improvisation

Through a 4-step process, you can develop skills in co-creating with spirit

Find tools in facing fears and the unknown

Develop skills in trusting and surrendering to the materials

Understand commonalities between creativity and spiritual principles

Learn about the cycles of the creative process

Develop awareness through the body and energetic practices

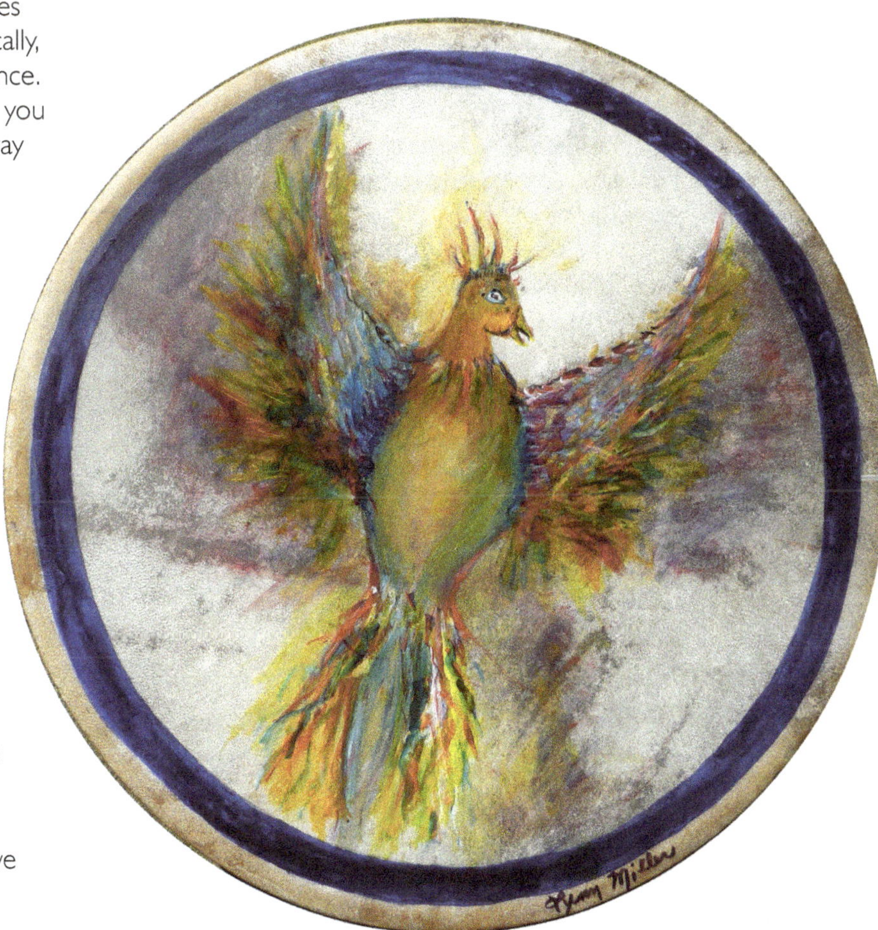

Phoenix Drum, Lynn Miller

Creativity, Improvisation and Spirit

Creativity is an integral part of every individual's ability to live a fulfilled life. The arts are a powerful catalyst for change – including spiritual awakening, personal growth, self-expression, healing, therapeutic processes, cultural awareness, and community building. Despite all the benefits from cultivating creativity, our culture does not always treat creativity as the foundation of our well-being.

Since our western society is thought-based, it identifies and values form. As a result, many have been influenced to believe that the material world of form is more important than the worlds of imagination or the unknown. Most of us were taught that the arts are not really relevant or serious and only for kids or talented ones. "Can you make money? If not, where is the value?"

These old belief patterns may stop us in our tracks. How many times have you felt, I must – clean the house, do my email, or a number of other chores – before I can create? Afterwards, you are just too tired to pursue your creativity. "Do your homework and put the crayons down." Is this an old voice of a parent or teacher? Once you bring mindful awareness to this old voice, you show that you are onto it. The voice will begin to lose its power as you learn to dis-identify from it and it will eventually disappear.

When I was in kindergarten, they used to give us modeling clay and crayons. Remember the glue we all tried to eat? Sadly they took our crayons away and gave us pencils and books. What would it be like if they hadn't taken the crayons away? S*pirtArts* is here to give you back the crayons. Once our imaginations are liberated, we all have the freedom to create.

The arts are for everyone. Even though we all have creative potential, few of us make use of our gift. *SpiritArts* provides tools to enter the creative process. You will be guided to explore dance, music, and visual art, regardless of your current level of experience. And yes, if you wish to, you can create in more than one art form. You have permission. In our compartmentalized society, we sometimes think we can do one thing only. However, once you develop a way to access one art form improvisationally, all the others can be approached in the same way. By exploring a theme auditorily, kinesthetically, and visually, the whole body is engaged, deepening the process and our understanding. When we express ourselves through our whole bodies, we become open to the opportunity of unique authentic expression. There is only one you. When we approach the arts improvisationally, we open doors of possibilities.

Improvisation is the method that can connect us to ***many*** art forms, to ourselves, and to something greater than ourselves. When we speak of improvisation, we are not describing only jazz or theater improvisation, with which many associate improvisation. In our context, improvisation is creating spontaneously in the moment. We are not able to see what is ahead. We face the unknown. When coming from ***nothingness***, we invite the Creative Source to work through us. There is an art to improvising; it is a practice. In order to have a successful improvisation, we must learn to get out of the way so that we may dance with the muse. ***SpiritArts*** will provide tools to develop improvisational skills in all art forms – including skills in facing a blank page; dancing from your soul; and singing or playing music without years of musical training or even knowing how to read music.

Spirituality is a connection to a higher power, a force greater than ourselves. This higher power is the Source of all things. Spirit is the non-physical part of you that has access to the wisdom of all that is. When you commit to self as spirit, spirit commits back to you and the magic begins. Alignment with spirit brings inspiration to create art, music, dance, drama, or poetry.

Children are fine examples: they come fresh from the Source, connected to spirit before societal programming. Most children are curious and ready to explore through color, form, movement, stories, and music. They are innately creative before societal conditioning of being told they are right or wrong.

Good/bad and right/wrong conditioning begins to block our awareness of this creative force. We begin to concern ourselves with, "Am I doing it right?" Our inner child begins to seek approval to be accepted. Many feel ashamed expressing themselves out of fear that they may look foolish. Meanwhile, the soul becomes smaller and unexpressed. The time has come to unblock that conditioning, to go within to rediscover your creative self and to restore your soul.

I invite you to be open to the possibilities, and to take a risk so that the magic can begin. You can live your creative dreams. It will not happen by waving a magic wand so your wishes will come true. The magic happens only by continuously showing up so that the universe knows you are ready. Trust and allow yourself to be guided. All you have to do is get out of your own way and be willing to take a risk. Anything is possible when you are open to it.

What Do Improvisation, Creativity and Spirituality Have in Common?

Approaching the arts improvisationally or in the moment, without a preconceived idea, communicates with spirit, since it is the language of the soul. Furthermore, the same principles apply to spiritual concepts, as well as to the process for creating improvisationally. The creative process and spirituality teach lessons in giving and receiving, deep listening, trusting, letting go, surrender, releasing judgment, being in the moment, and coming from love.

Therefore, creating from nothing – or improvisationally – gives you a playground to practice spiritual lessons. Improvising arts as a spiritual path is a practice and, even though it is spontaneous, it takes practice. Once your practice is developed through the arts, you will gain a better understanding of how spiritual principles work. This experience builds your confidence in applying these spiritual/improvisation principles through all of your life. If you learn to get out of your own way and listen deep, you will be guided. Life becomes art, and art becomes life.

Often profound answers lie in simplicity. Synchronicity is in sync with simplicity. If you apply improvisation principles to your whole life, you will attract synchronicity. Spiritual answers also lie in simplicity. Keep it simple. Living a spiritual path through art can promote a magical existence. Practicing art and integrating it in your life will reward you with a greater sense of fulfillment. Have fun.

SpiritArts 4-Step Process

How does one get started in creating art, music, or dance without a preconceived idea? How does one receive inspiration? When we are inspired, we are motivated with divine influence. The 4-step process contains four principles that comprise the thread to help connect us to inspiration. These key principles open the door to approach the arts in a moment-to-moment experience and open us to the flow. When we are in the flow, we are in a state of being fully engaged, energized, spontaneous, and aligned with spirit.

These 4 steps help us connect to inspiration or the flow state. They form the foundation for all the exercises in the book. Use these 4 steps when approaching all art forms and when doing any of the exercises in the book. They are the centering and reference points if you find yourself over-analyzing, needing to know, stuck, or uninspired.

Each step is described in detail, along with exercises. Practicing the ENERGY exercises helps your body remember. Eventually, your body will know and you will connect with the flow without preparing or thinking about it.

The 4-Step Process is:

1. *THE BREATH – connects to Spirit through the body.*
2. *BODY AWARENESS – ground, move out of thoughts into senses*
3. *HEART CONNECTION – connects body, mind, soul*
4. *DEEP LISTENING – silence to receive guidance*

Step 1: The Breath

Breath is the connection to Spirit

How does one be in the moment, let go of thoughts, give up control and fears in the mind? Through the breath. It reminds us of the present moment, to relax, to be in the now.

FOCUS YOUR ATTENTION ON YOUR BREATH. This will help you:

- Relax
- Center
- Connect with body
- Become present
- Connect with spirit

Our bodies voluntarily breathe for us. Even though we don't have to think about it, there are benefits to paying attention to our breath. Why breathe consciously?

Breathing is what keeps us alive. A breath is the difference between being dead and alive. A breath brings us the life force energy – Chi. The air we breathe connects us with everyone and everything. We all share the same air – recycling it – in and out. We breathe the same air that our ancestors breathed, connecting us to them. The Latin word for breath is spiritus (spirit) and the Latin word for spirit is spirare (to breathe). Breathing connects us to Spirit. Breathing connects us to all, oneness, all that there is.

Have you ever taken a deep conscious breath and noticed how it relaxes you? Many forms of meditation focus on breathing as a way to center and connect with body, mind, and spirit. When a deep breath is taken, it helps us to drop down into our bodies, quieting our minds.

A breath is the first physical act that we take on our own after leaving the womb. We come into this world naturally knowing how to breathe from the diaphragm. If you watch a baby breathe, their bellies go up and down. If you ask most adults to take a big breath, you may notice their shoulders go up and down. If someone's shoulders are moving up and down as they breathe, it indicates that they are breathing from their chest up. I call this "upside-down breathing" and have a theory why so many of us breathe from our chests. Growing up, we were taught to stand up straight, belly in, chest out (military stance). Try breathing in that posture. It teaches you to hold your breath and breathe from the chest. In Western culture, we spend much of the time in our thinking mind, not grounded in our bodies. We have a preoccupation with the external appearance of our bodies rather than the internal feeling of being within our bodies. Appearance may be another reason for upside-down breathing. The media influences women to hold in their bellies for good appearance. Such a posture will assure chest breathing. Another reason could be that, in the course of their lives, some people developed the fright/flight response to situations. With this response, the breath is taken in as a gasp. Try breathing in as a gasp. The air is taken in through the chest. This response to fear becomes the new learned way of breathing and creates shallow breathing. Fear is un-oxidated energy. Have you noticed, when under stress, that you may forget to breathe fully? Shallow breathing enables us to stuff our emotions. When you breathe fully, feelings that have been buried may surface. The solution is to breathe through them, so that they can move through and out.

Be aware of your breathing. It is something you can check at any moment – in the car, the grocery store, or at work. How are you breathing? Change begins with awareness. Take a moment, breathe.

Breathing from the diaphragm is the most beneficial way of breathing. It has many benefits including relaxation, oxygenating the cells in the body, connecting with feelings, staying in the present moment, and connecting with spirit. These benefits make it worthwhile to make a conscious effort to retrain your breathing habits. Even though it may take awhile and conscious effort, the payoffs are huge.

If this practice is new for your body, you may find yourself wanting to yawn afterwards. Your body is saying, "Yeah, let's have some more of this oxygen." If you do not usually breathe this way, you may feel light-headed. Can you feel your feet touching the ground? Focus your attention to your feet on the ground and stomp them a little.

Make conscious breathing a daily practice. Practice it when lying in bed in the morning or going to bed at night. This daily practice will help you sleep better and wake up more energized.

What does this all have to do with art? Conscious breathing widens your range of inner creative resources. When approaching each art form, begin with your breathing. Allow breath and body to guide you to the blank page, instrument, or movement. Your breath will help you to center and drop into your body; it increases your awareness and grounds you in the present moment. The mind loves to dwell in the past or future. You will be giving it a little break since spirit lives in the present moment.

Breath Exercises

Breath Awareness

Notice how you are breathing. What is happening in your body as you breathe? Where is your body rising and falling? Can you get a nice full breath in? Put your hands on your belly and behind your back. Is anything moving?

Diaphragm Breathing

Breathe in the nose and out the mouth. Breathing in through your nose, fill your belly with air like filling a big balloon. Put your hands on your belly to feel this motion. As you inhale, feel your belly going out. As you exhale through the mouth, notice that your belly goes in. Put your hands on the back and front of your torso. Feel your entire ribcage moving, your back, sides, as well as your belly. Slowly in and out, expand and contract.

On the exhale, purse your lips. Imagine sending just enough air to hold up a feather in front of your mouth. Not so much that you lose control of the feather or so little that the feather drops.

Breath Feedback

If you are having difficulty finding your belly place, lie on your back with a pillow under your knees. Put one hand on the chest and the other on the belly. On the inhale, feel your belly rise and notice your back pushing against the floor. Focus on moving the breath from your belly to your chest – like filling a barrel. Try to keep your shoulders from moving. Practice breathing slowly and evenly.

You can also get feedback by lying on the floor with your belly touching the floor. Use your elbows and forearms to hold up your chest. Breathe in through your nose, concentrating on filling your belly with air (inflate). Feel your belly pushing against the ground. Exhale through the mouth and feel your belly go in (deflate). Use the feedback from the floor as your belly pushes against it as a guide to re-training your body breath.

Breath painting

Drop a few splashes of water, color paints, or inks thinned with water on wet or dry paper. Using a blow pen or a straw, blow the colors around the paper. Send the spirit and breath into the colors. Observe your breath moving the colors. Watch the colors dance across the page. They always bring surprises – unplanned shapes, patterns, and designs.

Step 2: Body Awareness

Your body as a way of knowing

FOCUS YOUR ATTENTION ON YOUR BODY. This will help you:

- Relax
- Let go of thoughts
- Open your senses
- Ground

Our breath connects us with spirit that, in return, connects us to our bodies. Our inner wisdom and intuition dwells in our body, not in our analytical mind. The second step in awakening the creative spirit is to connect with the body.

This body awareness exercise grounds us to the earth and opens us to sky energy. Our body is a container between the sky and the earth. Combining earth and sky energies helps keep our container in balance.

Many people have disconnected from their bodies, which also cuts off the senses. When we are embodied, we are connected through our senses. Our senses – auditory, visual, and kinesthetic – can be expressed through visual art, music, poetry, storytelling, and movement.

When we arrived on this planet, we relied on our senses. We were attuned to them, ready to listen and explore. Watch a baby or toddler exploring the space around them – wide-eyed, finding magic in everything they see. Practice looking at everyone or everything as if for the first time – wide-eyed, big breath, ahhhh. Make an art out of seeing and hearing as if for the first time.

As we became educated and socialized, many of us lost our body connections. We were taught to follow our minds. As members of an advanced society, the intellect was given more value than our own innate wisdom. Therefore, many people lost touch with this wisdom – our body's own wisdom. We have an inner wisdom that is often not heard above our internal chatter. There is an innate intelligence – an inner voice – underneath the small talk, worrying, and judgmental voices.

Body, mind, and spirit connect by exploring through the senses, rather than solely by thinking our way toward a solution. Cognitive reasoning serves a purpose, but it can grow out of balance. Don't give up on the mind; just don't let it control you. Give the body and spirit equal attention.

Make the art of seeing, hearing, feeling, moving, and listening a daily practice. Your perspective may begin to change.

Body Awareness Exercises

Centering

Breathe, focus your attention in your body. While standing, bend your knees slightly in an athletic stance, with your feet firmly placed on the ground. Imagine a magnet planting them into the earth. Feel the support and strength of the earth. Breathe in from the ground, expanding your belly, moving the energy through your body, up to the crown of your head. Imagine a string from the wisdom above opening the top of your head. Exhale from your crown, moving energy down to your feet. Repeat several cycles. You can also be sitting while you do this exercise.

Sensory Walk

When going for a walk, notice the colors, shapes, and sounds around you. Look up to the sky, at the infinite. Observe details: the inside of a flower, a pinecone. See the shapes and patterns in the landscape. Notice how your feet feel on the ground. Move your body in different ways. Listen to your steps, your rhythm, the rhythms around you. How many different sounds can you hear? Now, listen to the silence. Breathe.

Opening Senses

Shut your eyes. Connect with your senses. Notice your breath. Feel yourself sitting in the chair. Notice where your body meets the chair. Feel your feet on the ground.

Auditory sense: *What do you hear? Listen to the sounds around you. Listen to the rhythm. Do you hear a melody or rhythmic pattern from the birds, cars, hammering, talking, fan, or whatever sounds are in your environment? Slowly open your eyes.*

Visual senses: *What is around you? Look around the room with wonderment, as if you are seeing it for the first time. Focus on the things around you – the patterns, rhythms, colors, shapes, and shadows.*

Movement senses: *How does your body feel sitting in the chair? Slowly stand up, begin walking and moving in space. Notice your feet on the ground. Notice the rhythm of your pace as well as the sound that your feet make on the ground. Open the crown of your head while you feel your feet on the ground. Notice the spaces above you, below you, in front of you, behind you. Observe how you feel inside.*

Step 3: Connect with the Heart

Follow your heart

FOCUS YOUR ATTENTION ON YOUR HEART. This will help you:

- Follow your intuition
- Move out of linear thinking
- Connect with soul
- Expand consciousness
- Be compassionate

Our heart has intuitive intelligence; its scope exceeds the linear thinking of our brain. The heart is the connector of the body, mind and soul. The heart is multi-dimensional – it communicates with the soul and is the voice of the higher self. It also communicates with the body and calms the mind. Listen to your heart for guidance. Loving acceptance of the heart opens one to this spiritual source.

Bringing conscious attention to the heart allows the soul to let its energy flow and create through the individual. This is co-creation. Your soul is part of you. Soul brings more energy to you when you direct more energy toward it. The heart has a wisdom, an intelligence.

> "Your body does meet your soul. They directly connect in your deep heart, in the energy center just above the base of your sternum. Here, near the core of your body, rests a point of interface between your physical being and your purely transcendent self (Frediani p. 5).

When we come from our mind, we carry polarities, good and bad. When we come from the heart, we carry wisdom and love. When we are heart-focused, we display compassion.

Focusing on the heart gives you knowledge that the greatest good is coming. This knowledge can produce joyous feelings of gratitude. Give gratitude for what you do have – the gifts and miracles that you have already been given. Don't judge or compare your own unique abilities – to move, see, make sounds, play music – with others. Be happy if you are able make a sound, see, or move. We are all unique and special. Gratitude helps silence the judging mind and keeps us feeling positive.

Approach your art with gratitude. Practice connecting with your heart, create a relationship with your heart. Spend a week connecting with your heart and feeling gratitude. Notice anything different?

Doc Childre is the founder of Heart Math, a research group that has proven that the heart has its own brain and that it generates the largest energy field of any organ in the body. The heart sends a message to the brain, quieting the thoughts and bringing new insights. When we expand our heart center, we expand our consciousness and centeredness.

Listen from your heart. Shift your focus from your head to your heart. Your heart is in the center of the body. Your body is in the center between the heavens and the earth. The heart is connected with the center of all things.

Heart Exercises

Awakening the Heart Center

Breathe into your heart while expanding your belly. Bring focused energy toward your heart. Can you feel sensations or energy moving? Focus with the intention, "I am connecting with my heart."

Gratitude Chant

Start with the breath. Breathe into the heart. Complete these sentences with a movement, gesture, phrase, or song expressing gratitude.

I am grateful for-------------------------------

I give thanks for-------------------------------

Heart Breath

Make time each day to sit quietly and focus in your heart. Imagine you are breathing through your heart while expanding your belly on inhale. Calm your mind. Try to not think of anything but breathing through your heart. When your mind is clear, you will begin to receive impressions and ideas. These are coming from your heart. Pay attention.

Heaven and Earth Breath

On the inhale, breathe into your heart. Imagine energy simultaneously going to the feet and the crown, gathering wisdom from the heavens and the earth. On the exhale, imagine energy from the feet and crown going out through the heart. Do several cycles of this breathing.

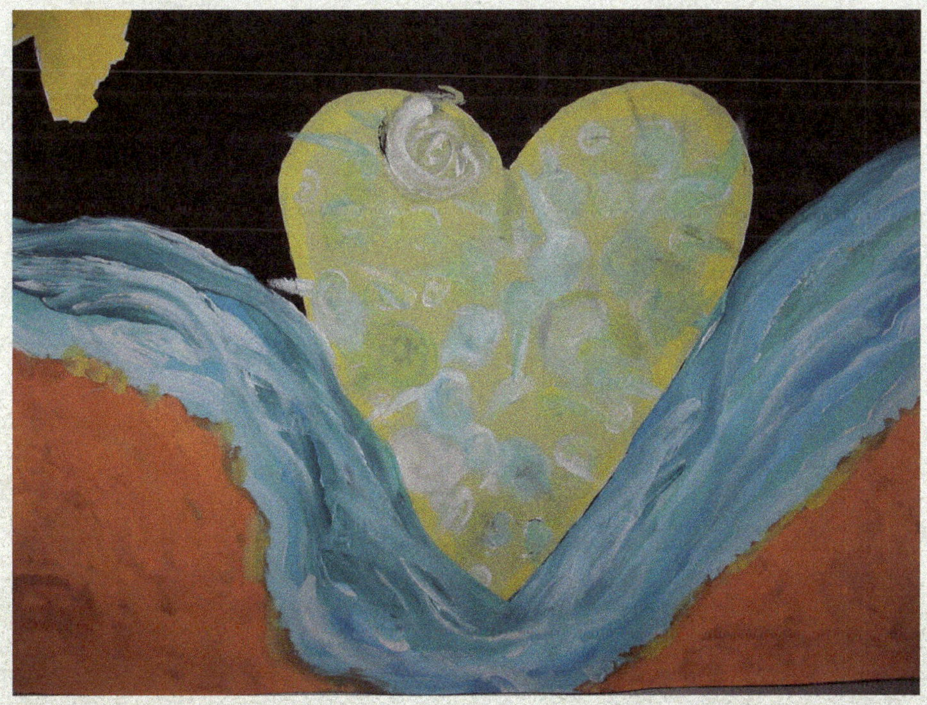

Heart opening, anonymous

Step 4: Deep Listening

Listen to the stillness, where all creation originates

In this exploration using song, dance, and the visual arts, direction comes from an inner knowledge obtained by quieting the mind. Creativity is born in stillness. Begin with silence that centers you with the force of all things. Be fully attentive and focused; listen with your whole body and not just your ears. Wait for an impulse. Impulses are vibrations of energy that guide us. When we truly listen, our vibration becomes aligned with this force. There is power in stillness and in silence. They are where you will hear your inner knowledge and be guided.

The creative spirit is in the present moment. Inner wisdom can be heard in stillness. Some may have become more disconnected from their inner spirit and are more connected with their thoughts. Creation comes from emptiness, when the chatter stops. Even a gentle hum can stop the chatter and connect you to the Source.

When you do this humming exercise, you are vibrating your body. You are creating movement, movement away from the mind. It is near impossible to keep thoughts going when focused on humming. Where do you feel it? What do you notice?

Deep listening is listening unconditionally, opening to awareness within. When you receive an impulse or guidance, act on it. Don't analyze or let your mind talk by telling you, "You are not ready. You are not good enough … not trained enough … not talented enough."

Surrender to the force, let go of control. Be willing to take a risk and show up. Be courageous. Westerners tend to look at surrender as defeat. It is really letting go, allowing yourself to be all you can be. Spirit has no limits–ANYTHING IS POSSIBLE when you are open to it. Say "Yes!" to your music, life, and art. When you say yes, you open to possibilities, align your energy, and your vibrations. Allowing helps you give up ego control.

Listen to the silence. Wait for an impulse. Catch the moment.

The 4-Step Process Summary

The energetic exercises described in the 4-step process help to bring awareness to your body, mind, and spirit in preparation for co-creation. Depending on where you are on your journey, you may require more or less practice. Once you begin to connect, you are ready to move through the steps in one flow.

1. BREATH. Feel your feet on the ground and breathe.

2. BODY. Notice body sensations, connect in body. If you are not connecting, go back to the breath. Repeat the process. Connect with the body, through gentle movements, ground.

3. HEART. Connect in the heart through the breath.

4. LISTEN for opportunity and take it.

If you practice the 4-step process when approaching the arts, creativity will flow. The following chapters will give more insight on how to begin creating authentically. Whether a song, dance, or visual art, the path to creating authentically is through improvisation – the process for meeting the creative spirit within.

Listening Exercises

Inner Connection

Enter nature -- listen to the birds, the wind, a trickling brook. You can see, hear, and feel the Source. Recognizing this communion can bring inner peace.

Resonance Hum

Create an intention such as, "I am connecting with my creative spirit." Then take three deep breaths and make a gentle hum, noticing where you feel it in your body. After this humming exploration, listen to the silence.

Allow Chant

Begin with the breath, connect in the body. Sit in stillness. Listen. Go back to the breath, the body, and chant slowly the word "allow." Draw out the vowel sounds. "aaahhhhhlllllllooooooowwwwwwwwwww…" Repeat. Sit in silence.

Co-creating through 4-Step Process

While standing, bend your knees slightly in an athletic stance with your feet firmly placed on the ground. If sitting, notice where you are touching the chair. Breathe. Focus your attention in your body. Let your body sway. Breathe into your heart. Feel lifted by your crown. Listen. If you have an impulse, take it! Do not censor. Begin with a note, a brush stroke, a movement. This is your creative beginning.

Spirit of Improvisation

Improvisation is creating in the moment

Improvising is creating spontaneously. It is dancing in the moment with the unknown. It is active participation, not watching someone else or having someone else make it up for you. It is your expression or creation from within. It can be done by yourself or with others. It is unique in the moment. It is the courage to be authentic.

How do you learn how to improvise? You improvise by stepping out of your own way and trusting the unknown. Begin with the 4-step process: breath, body awareness, opening your heart, and listening for guidance. Following this process will create presence.

To improvise, one must let go of thoughts. "For art to appear, we have to disappear" (Nachmanovitch, p. 51). After giving up control, we must trust the process. This requires being in the moment, fully in the experience. Authentic creative expression comes through in present time only. When we accept where we are without an agenda, we are a vessel for the creative spirit to move through, and for creative expression to emerge.

The creative outcome feels like something beyond self, something for which you cannot take credit. This experience is co-creation. It teaches one to trust in something larger than oneself. Improvising is listening to the inner voice or intuitive self that guides us, and acting on it. It produces pure inspiration. When we are in the flow, creativity is effortless. You only need to relax. Breathe, stay in body, have fun, listen, and dance with the muse. In order to re-program what we have learned from coming into adulthood, this process requires practice.

If it is so easy, why is it so hard? If someone asks you to sing a solo, it can feel like a life and death situation. Your heart may begin to race and fear begins. Why are we embarrassed to sing, dance, and be playful? Are there feelings of shame, not being good enough, fear of failure, looking foolish, or fear of the unknown? In our ego-based training into adulthood, our mind-self wants to position itself to appear good. In order to be accepted, most of us learned this lesson as children. If we feel we have failed or not done well enough, we feel ashamed and depressed.

We are more than the mask that wants to be perfect. Underneath is our true essence, our soul. Images, music, and dance are the language of the soul. Creating spontaneously originates from this true essence. "What we have to express is already in us, so the work of creativity is not a matter of making the material come, but unblocking the obstacles to its natural flow" (Nachmanovitch p.10).

Obstacles are what block creativity. They develop when we are not in the moment but, instead, are in our head – worrying about not being accepted, not being good enough, wondering if they like it – I'll show them; I'm the best. The key to authenticity is to remove those obstacles by stepping out of your own way. When we talk about improvisation or deep listening, we also need to address the obstacles, for they are intertwined.

Obstacles: Facing Fears

Know fearlessness by going into the fear

Most of us carry fears. It is part of being human. Many received negative patterning from their family of origin, education system, or other authority figures. Someone might have manipulated us to fit into what they wanted us to be, not who we really are. Often, we then assume the role of being our own judge and critic. "Hey, do something worthwhile. You are not good at that. You don't have time for that." Whose voice is this? We use our own voice and actions to prolong the negative influences of that person or situation. Do you really want to continue to be controlled by false beliefs and patterns from childhood? Try this adapted Qigong exercise.

Fear blocks the creative flow. It is one of our biggest obstacles. Fear of being wrong, fear of failure, fear of success, or the unknown are defenses against creativity and spontaneity. We must first acknowledge our fears in order to face them. Fear arises from sensing the presence of danger whether real or imagined.

When we look at fear right in the eye, it won't seem so big. When we can see it, move it, or hear it, we may then recognize when we allow negativity into our imagination. If allowed to accumulate, fear will block the flow of our creative energy.

Be aware of being afraid to fail. Fear of failure can drive us into doubtfulness, indecision, or pursuit of perfection. When we are too concerned with being good or right, it stops the creative flow. We enter into a drama or control mode, and forget to listen or trust our Source. So-called failing can open us to new ways of thinking and new possibilities, or direct us toward ways we can improve.

You can break these cycles by not taking yourself too seriously. If you discover yourself overly burdened and concerned with getting it right, laugh. Fear does not like to be laughed at. It wants to be taken very seriously. Smiling and laughter will support you in lightness of being. When you laugh, you are calling spirit. It fills the body with air and oxygen. Laughing brings in life force energy. It releases energy that is stuck, bringing movement toward possibilities. Practice laughing. Laugh out loud. You may have to fake it at first, then it will come. What does it sound like, feel like? It is contagious. We all have our own unique sound of laughter. It is important to laugh at oneself, and not take life situations so seriously. Smiling and laughing help us release endorphins and feel positive.

Facing your Fears

Put the past behind you

Slowly turn your head to the right moving your eyes as far as they can see. Affirm, "I love and leave the past behind me." Slowly turn your head to the left moving with your eyes affirming, "I love and leave the past behind me." Repeat several times, and do this often to clear past energy.

What does fear look like?

Take out a blank sheet of paper and some oil pastels. Connect with fear in your body. What does it feel like, look like? Choose a color and express the feeling on paper. Pay attention to your body's response when you come from a place of fear. Give your picture a title.

What does fear feel like?

Connect with your feelings of fear. Where is it located? Feel its texture, express it, mime it. Let the feelings move through your body; then release them. Shake them off.

What does fear sound like?

With your voice or an instrument, create the sound of fear. Do not censor.

Smiling Meditation

Take three deep cleansing breaths in the nose and out the mouth. Feel your feet on the ground. Open your crown above the top of your head. Imagine an inner smile on your forehead. Feel a lift. Slowly move the smile down your nose to your mouth. Smile at your ears. Thank all these parts as you smile at them. Smile at your throat, your chest, and into your heart. Give thanks for all these parts. Smile into your solar plexus, your lower belly, and where your body meets the chair. Say I love you. Smile into your thighs, your calves and at your feet. Say thank you.

Cultivating Awareness

Listen to your thoughts

All change begins with awareness. Notice your thoughts. Do not give them a lot of attention. "I hear you. Oh yes, there you are again." Thoughts are only thoughts. There is no need to hold onto a thought, or to become attached to it. You can transcend negativity by watching and observing thoughts without judgment.

It is important to change negative self-talk to positive self-talk. Positive affirmations are helpful in deprogramming negativity. An affirmation is a positive statement spoken in the present tense. Try it, whether you believe it or not. An example would be, "I feel good about myself." "I have a great voice. It is unique, not like anyone else's." Affirm the statement in the present.

You may have to state your affirmations over and over to change the old programming in your mind. It is also helpful to put these statements in writing. When you free your negative thoughts and beliefs, you free your life force energy for creativity. Our thoughts, feelings, and opinions create the experiences in our lives. Your world will reflect what you say, so be aware of what you are saying to yourself!

Clearing obstacles is a process. When we lead from our mind (negative ego), we position ourselves to seek approval, to be on top, and to stay in control. When we lead from our heart, we connect with spirit within. Silence is our friend when walk into the unknown, listening for guidance.

Love your negativity

When you have a negative thought, play this game:

I hear that negative self. Acknowledge it, it is a wounded part. Say to yourself, "I love you." Make it a game. When you catch it, it loses its importance and disappears. Breathe deeply, and come back to the present moment. Coming back into your body and feeling sensations will distract your mind.

Facing the Unknown

Creative force lives in the unknown

Trusting Intuition

Engage the 4-step process of connecting into body through breath and breathing into the heart. Still and quiet the mind. You may ask yourself questions, listen for the answer. Listen to what you hear and trust it. Write them down in your journal. Follow through on your messages.

Do not be afraid of the silence, the emptiness, the not knowing. Creativity arises in the emptiness, the not knowing. In our linear training, we have been taught to want to know: analyze, name, categorize, prove, and control. Imagination, magic, and intuition have been labeled as suspicious. Yet what a magical mystery life is. The major forces in our lives are unknowns. Sometimes we fear what we can not see. Western culture is analytical, holding onto what is real, what can be proved, what can be measured. Do we disregard the magic, the intuitive, the creative, or the imagination because we fear the unknown?

In a quest to be normal, many people have lost touch with their creative selves. They have shut down their imagination and learned not to listen to their intuition. With reason qualifying a person's ability to adapt to reality, we have made fantasy and imagination unlikely to be considered normal. Our tribe or culture does not often encourage us to be creative free thinkers. Demands and expectations are put on us through families of origins, school, or church. Wanting to be accepted and meet expectations, many abandon their dreams and authentic selves.

Despite our background in linear reality, every night we enter into a dream world. In the non-linear dream world, our soul attempts to communicate with us through symbols and images. Since we experience this realm every night, we have nothing to fear from it. Many indigenous peoples believe the dream world is the real world, and our waking world is the dream.

When we walk into the unknown, we develop our inner knowing, opening our dimensions and vision. When you get an inner message or gut feeling, honor it. Find delight in being able to see more than what is in front of you. We all have this gift; we just need to cultivate it.

Respect your imagination. Many will say, "Oh, it was ***just*** my imagination, I didn't ***know*** what I was doing." It is through not knowing that we discover imagination.

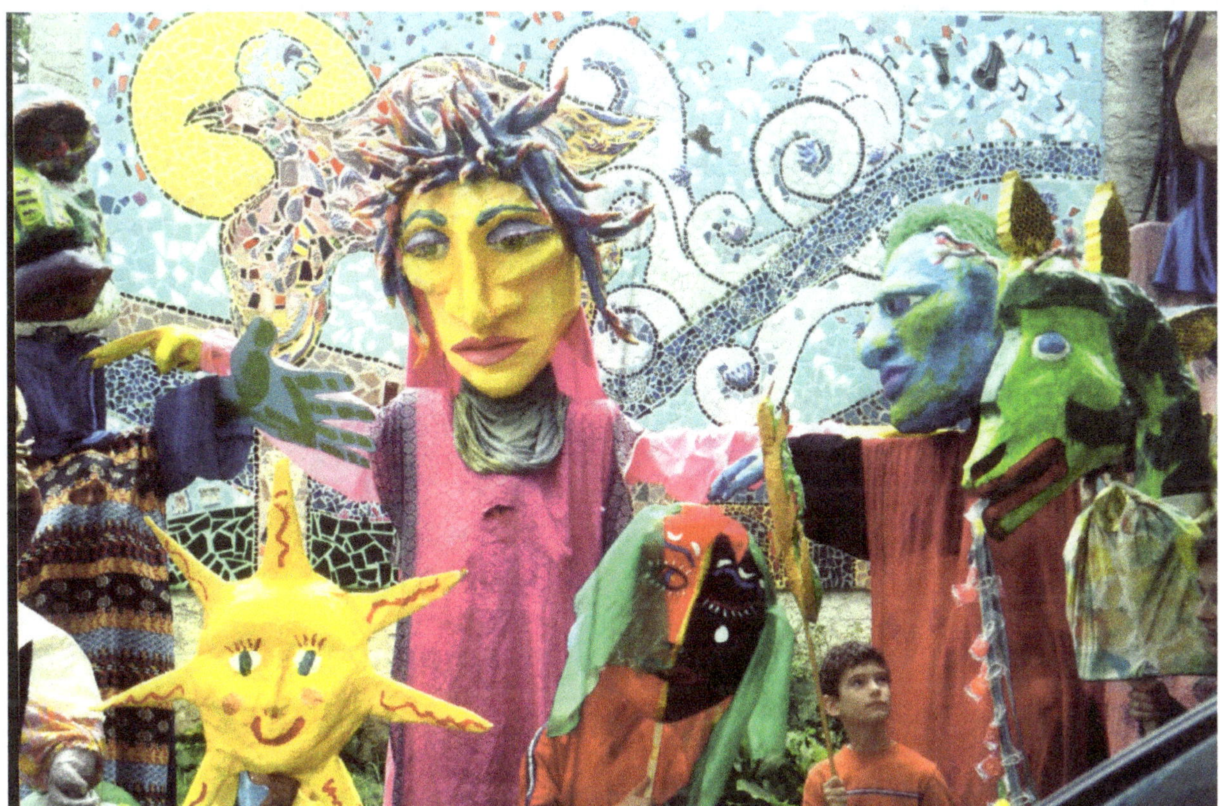

Giant Puppets and Mural - photo by Peter Bruchner

When we go into a relaxed state and just write freely, we can uncover thoughts and feelings through fantasy. When we open the imagination, we visit what is in our subconscious. We become conscious by making what is unconscious, conscious. When we have consciousness, we have awareness. When we are aware, we become open to a bigger picture, adding new dimensions and wisdom. What we can see and what we cannot see are of equal importance. There is a web of energy – called life force energy – that connects both worlds. Everything is energy: humans, plants, animals, rocks. Our spirit or soul is energy. As we awaken, we feel or see the life force within us and all things, and how we are all connected. When we open to the intangible realm, we allow a relationship with spirit.

Honor and respect the spirit that is in everything. Animals, plants, and crystals are especially connected to us and are here to help us. A child with an active imagination talks with its stuffed animals as if they were real. They are real; everything has a soul. This concept is taught in Native American teachings and much of Eastern thought. More people are opening to their intuition – which is trusting the imagination.

Creating with natural materials such as sticks, stones, tree bark, and grasses is a great way to open the imagination and to open to creative spirit. The creative spirit lives in nature. Allow the imagination; bring back the fantasy; stay open to your dreams. Don't discard these jewels when they come to you. They are all found in the not knowing.

Imagination Exercises

Opening Imagination

Shut your eyes; follow your breath until you are relaxed. Imagine a beautiful place in nature. Imagine what it looks like, feels like. You are moving freely, dancing with nature, singing with the birds, playing with the animals. Imagine yourself rolling on the ground, feel the grass, the earth. Once you have played enough, come back to stillness, the breath. When you are ready, slowly open your eyes.

With pen and paper begin writing without stopping, beginning with, "Once upon a time." Do not be concerned if you are making sense, just keep writing until you come to the end.

Believing Imagination

Enter into nature and collect some stones. Ask them if it is OK to take them home or to play with them where you found them. Create a relationship with the stones. Rub them and feel their textures. They like having attention, just as you do. Hit two stones together. What does it sound like? Rub them together. What does that sound like? Make a rhythmic pattern, and sing with them. Make a design with them. What kind of shapes can you make, such as a circle or crescent?

Pick up a stone and ask it if it has anything to tell you. Don't censor. You may be surprised with the wisdom of the stone.

Develop Imagination

Look around the room and personify objects around you. They are made from energy and vibrations just like you. Talk to them as if they are your friends or angels. Talk to the plant, the sculpture, the chair. Ask them a question. Listen for an answer.

Nature Ritual

Go for a walk in nature. Collect shapes and textures such as tree bark, limbs, leaves, grasses, stones. With twine, wire, or other fasteners, combine the gifts you find. You may add paint, feathers, or any other materials you have at home. The result may end up 2-dimensional or 3-dimensional. If you can pick it up, dance with it. If it is flat, dance to it. Move with abandon, connecting to the earth. Sing, dance, pray – honoring the mother.

Seeing the Infinite

Shut your eyes. What do you see? Is it just black? Where is this place? Is it space? Look into the infinite. Do you see speckles of color or light in the darkness? Look deeper. Are you afraid or, comforted with, this vastness right behind your own eyelids? Breathe. Don't fear going deeper.

This ritual will help you feel connected, held. The earth wants to be loved, acknowledged, and respected, just as we do. We are changing from a culture that had an attitude of conquering nature. If we do this, we will conquer ourselves. The more we are in relationship with our environment, such as the sun and moon, the more we open to a force larger than ourselves. As we open to more possibilities than our material world, we open our vision.

You will develop more belief in universal intelligence once you have less fear of the unknown, your imagination and intuitive powers. Open yourself to the infinite. Relinquish the need to know by surrendering to the moment. Breathe-ground-connect to body. Have reverence for the unknown. Cherish the moment. Have the courage to break old known patterns in exchange for growing through joy.

Cultivating Joy

Staying present in the moment, observing your thoughts and feelings, and staying non- judgmental are the recipe toward how much joy you can allow to flow. When you release fear of change, the magic begins to happen. You will feel connected, more alive, vital and spiritually in tune with life. The only thing we can really count on is change.

What is joy? Joy is when you are in your power. Power comes through by telling the truth, what you really feel. Joy is when you feel connected, when you feel love flowing. Joy is acceptance and surrender. What is joy to you? What brings you joy? Joy comes from the inside, not the outside. Joy is when we feel connected to our feelings, connected to ourselves, to others, to our dreams, and to the creator. Joy is when we feel the flow.

See yourself creating. Have you ever had a dream where you heard the most amazing music, or saw yourself dancing or flying? Okay, you feel the excitement and you want to create. But how does one start?

Connecting with Joy

Breathe in the nose and out the mouth. Connect with the body. Imagine being filled with joy. What does it feel like? How much joy can you bring in? Fill yourself with joy, allowing it to move through you. Imagine dancing, singing, and creating art with joy.

Surrender: Let the Materials Guide You

One mark, one note, or one gesture opens to a composition with infinite possibilities

How do I face a blank page? How do I write a song? How do I begin my dance? Even though the origin of inspiration seems to be a mystery, it comes from the space that is formless. Facing a blank page can feel like a void. Approach it with abandon, like a child. Begin with the 4-step process. Always start with the breath. Feel your feet on the ground, be alert as in an athletic stance, knees bent. Connect with your sensations. Begin moving, swaying until you feel impelled to go to the material – whether it be paint, clay, found objects, an instrument, your voice, body, paper and pen. Go to the material that is calling you. When you feel it, jump on board. Don't hesitate, you may risk going into judgment or monkeys of the mind.

"How do I choose the material or art form?" Listen. How do you feel right now? What is your sensory art form, or modality? Do you feel like: "I have to ***move*** through this"…."I need to ***grasp*** this"…."I don't ***hear*** myself"…."I **see** what you mean." The metaphor such as see, hear, or move gives a clue as to what art form to choose when listening to yourself or working with a client. Do you need color – a 3D quality? Do you need to move energy or sound it out? Do you want watercolors for more flow or to release grief? I need something solid; I want to work in concrete.

So now that an art form has been chosen, it is time to learn about its world. Discovering techniques of what the material can and cannot do is a new learning opportunity. Let the material guide you. Discover: What can the material do? You are not mastering the instrument, paint, or clay. You are working with it, playing with it, and dancing with it. There is a secret life in the material – a personality and a life of its own. Find the flow.

When we work with the material, we learn about different elements such as wood, air, metal. When we are in fear we may try to force our way through the experience. When we force, we approach the materials, instrument or art form through our mind and it is like we are trying to conquer it. When you come from the breath, you send spirit into the material. The spirit creates the form.

Each of us will have our own unique sense of style, design choice, and preference. The particular material you have chosen is already resonating with you symbolically.

Let's say you have chosen your voice. Surrender to the sound. Begin with one note, really listen, and it will take you to the next. Surrender to the note. Don't try to control it; play with it. What can it do? How high can it go? How low? What can it do? What styles or textures might it sound like? Can you make it nasal, breathy, rhythmic?

If you chose a 3D art form, can it stand up? Surrender to the materials. Be curious, and let the material show you. Don't try to force it, or it may break the flow. What will help support it?

If you chose your body, begin with one gesture or repetitive movement. What can it do? Where does the movement want to go? You follow your body rather than your body following your mind. Surrender. Does it want to spin, balance itself, or stand up on the toes?

Working with the materials can teach us to let go, give up control. Breathe, surrender, allow. We know internally; if we listen, we will be guided.

Example: I wanted to paint a face of a goddess. No matter how much I tried to force this image, it looked like an old lady. I finally gave it up and went with the old lady image. I wanted her to be pretty, but there was something else that was trying to be expressed. If the material wants to do something, go with it. Metaphorically the old lady image appeared to show me something. After working with the image, she showed me that I was hiding behind perfectionism. I was trying to make things look good when I wasn't really feeling that way. (Later on in this book, I will explain more on how to work with your images).

Once I made a figure out of clay, but it would not stand up. The figure kept drooping over. I put sticks in the legs to reinforce it, but it continued to fall over. The material was teaching me about standing up, how to ground. I added more clay and gave it roots.

Begin with a scribble

With markers, oil pastels, or paint, move your arms as if painting in the air. Move your whole body, find the flow. Now dance with your paintbrush on the paper. Make scribbles, make sounds with your scribbles, or notice the sounds of the brush moving across the paper. Look at the shapes: what do you see? Draw out the detail, or fill in shapes with color.

Love Your Art, Your Art Loves You

Sounds are not right and wrong; they just are.

Once you have created a piece of art, music, dance, or writing, treat it as a friend. Do not judge it even if you are disappointed by the results. Have empathy for the piece if you think it is grotesque, ugly, lifeless. It is an expression of part of you and something greater than self, working together to bring you a gift. Some arts expressions come from our subconscious with messages to tell. Sometimes they want to show us something we would rather hide from, such as our shadow. Sometimes the messages will come to us later or on another level. Sometimes they are there for us not to know, especially if we live our lives always needing to know.

To honor your art in any modality, look and listen to the detail through shapes, lines, textures, space, dynamics, composition. The composition, colors, shapes, and sounds may give you inspiration for the next piece.

Check in with your body. How does it make you feel? Is it stirring up something that needs to be looked at? Does it calm you? Does it feel flat? If you have an uneasy feeling, there is probably something hiding that wants to be revealed or given attention. If it is flat, it may be a message to you to take more risks; you may be playing it too safe. Do something bodacious. Paint with a broom; play some pots and pans in the kitchen; jump up and down; yell, laugh, cry. If you love it, thank the muse. Now you are working in concert with the muse.

You just played something on your instrument. It is not the note that you wanted to hear. State it again as if you mean it. You may be only a half step away from where you wanted it to resolve; slide it there. Dissonant sounds can be exciting, interesting, create tension, release, resolve. Possibly what you thought was a mistake can open you up to something you would never have thought of. Embrace it, explore it, move with it.

When working on a visual art piece, don't be afraid that you will make a mistake and ruin what you started. Sometimes we create something and like it, but are afraid to move on. This feeling may keep your painting or drawing restricted to a specific manner.

If a spill or blob of color comes imperfectly off your brush, go with this new splash of color to see what it brings to you. It can move you toward another layer in your subconscious, open up new territories, or take you out of the box in a new direction.

Create a relationship with your art. It is not finished after the product has appeared.

Talk out loud to it as if you were talking to a friend or to a family member. Ask it questions. Give it thanks. Be grateful for where you are in the moment. Your art wants to be seen and heard just like you. Your Divine self will give you the answers metaphorically through the art. All you have to do is ask, then listen.

If we follow laws of spirituality in the process of authentic creativity, we will be guided. We will explore the laws or principles of spirituality and its relationship to the creative process.

Color Dance Exercise

Color Dance

With oil pastels, paints, or colored pencils, sit in front of a blank page. Play with the excitement of the unknown. Feel this in your body. Like a child: Wow! Rub your hands on the paper. Listen to the sound. Look at the colors as if you have never seen them before: Wow, blue, red! Move the colors on the blank page. Notice how they move on the paper; get into the way it feels as they move. Wow, the excitement of the unknown! Where will they move to next? Notice your body's response when you come from wonderment.

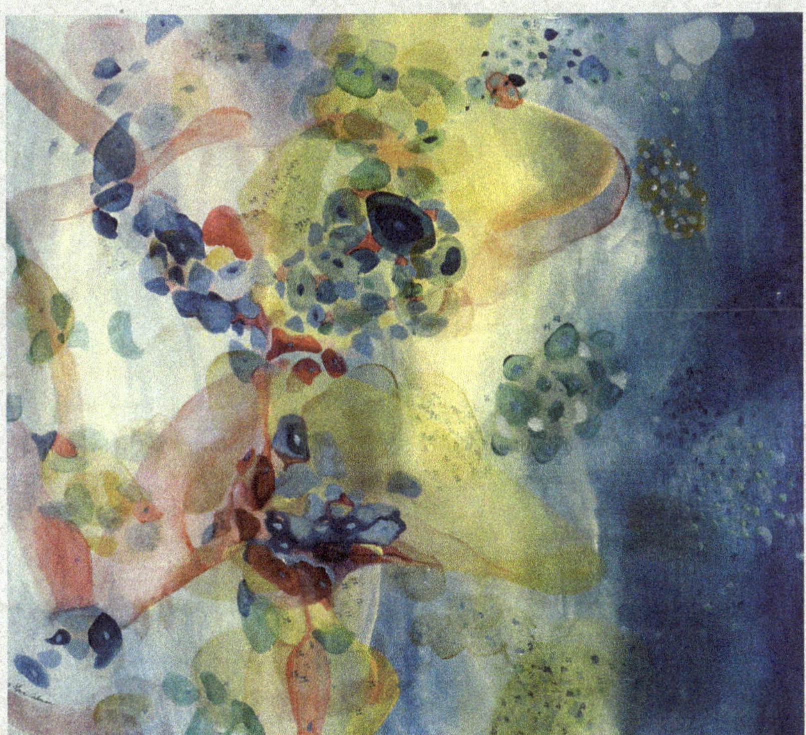

H2O Fantasy painting by Lynn MIller

Spirituality and the Creative Process

Many basic spiritual principles are the same principles in approaching art improvisationally, in the moment. The following is a step-wise account of how to create authentically, reviewing some of the concepts presented. Review this chart often to help remember. We begin with a desire. You may receive a feeling – a message from the muse. You might thwart that message and rationalize that it would not be practical (this is your mind speaking). Timing is everything and you may not feel ready. If you decide to follow through, this is the process:

SHOW UP

Say "yes" to your creative self. It is not going to happen unless you take some action. You may have plenty of desire but manifestation will not happen until you show the universe you want to do this. Be willing to take a risk. Give yourself permission and do it!

GROUND

Ground yourself and begin with the 4-step process: breath, body connection, and deep listening. This is an invitation to join with the muse. Remember: you don't have to take all the responsibility. The muse is happy to join you. Just ask. It is important to be grounded when exploring new dimensions.

POWER IN STILLNESS

Listen, silence is your friend. You are connected and can be guided if you listen. Stop thinking, connect with body sensations, feel your feet on the ground. Make friends with the unknown.

DETACHMENT

Let go of outcomes: Is it going to be good? Is it going to make me money? Approach your art with nothing to gain and nothing to lose. Abandon hope and fear. Focus on the process, the now moment, not the end product or result. Imagine a world with no good or bad. Everything just is. Wow, it feels simpler. What is good or bad, according to whom? Is there really a good or bad? Remember these are just labels. Whom do they serve?

OPEN YOUR HEART

Love and accept where you are – it's you! You may want to chant "Ahh" or "I AM." This will help to connect with your inner knowledge, clear the energy in the room, and connect with the infinite. Breathe into your heart, feel it pulsing – know you are one with the Source.

SURRENDER

Surrender to the moment. Surrender to the outcome, the materials, and to the process. Get out of your own way. Realize there is something greater than yourself you can co-create with. You don't have to do it all. You can ask for help. Your helpers are waiting standby. Let go, let God.

BE PRESENT

Do not be concerned with the end. If you are thinking of the past or future, you are not in the present moment. Make each moment so intriguing that it leads to the next note, color, movement.

PLAY

This is the free spirit of exploration. Return to the magical child; your inner spirit likes to play. Go back to this essence; your inner child was the first voice of inner knowing. Play with the colors, the sound, the movements. If you find yourself too serious – laugh.

Creative Exercises

Yes!

Practice saying yes. Walk around the room saying "YES." How does that feel? Now walk around saying, "No, I can't do that now." How does that feel? Now go back to saying yes, imagine yourself doing it – singing, dancing – whatever the desire is. Say yes! Call it out loud," YES, I can do this. I may never have done it but I can do it!"

Ground like Trees

Look at trees. Study their roots. Imagine what they look like under the ground. Imagine roots going into the ground from the bottom of your feet. Breathe, bend your knees in a ready position yet flexible to go with the flow.

Friends with the Unknown

Say out loud, "I am making friends with the unknown." It is exciting to see what will unfold next without knowing ahead of time. The unknown is safe. I am not alone in the unknown. I have the muse to help me. Listen for the muse.

Create with Detachment

Recite the mantra, "I have nothing to lose and nothing to gain. I am complete just as I am." The breath will help bring you to the present moment.

Put your hands over your heart. Breathe into your hands; give a hum with the intention of love. Open the hum to an Ahhh. Breathe, expand your arms, opening out then bring hands back to heart. Breathe, repeat several times. This opens the flow.

After opening your heart, call the muse. Ask for assistance in letting go to be guided. Always thank the muse afterward. Thank you, thank you, thank you.

The breath will bring you back to the present moment. Focus on your breath.

Start laughing if you notice yourself getting overly concerned. Can I do this? I don't have time for this. Stop, look at the colors, textures, sounds around you. Watch the shapes in the clouds, listen to the rhythms of the cars going by. Use this for inspiration. Find the joy around you. Be the joy.

Creative Exercises

Connect with Who You Really Are

Imagine an infinity sign in your jaw area. Image this sign repetitively circling over and over. Can you notice any loosening, unraveling. Now image this infinity sign moving down your body. Across your throat, chest, heart, solar plexus, belly, genitals, legs, feet. Now bring this infinity sign slowly back up out the top of your head. Breathe....

Imagine having the courage to tell the truth at all times. Say what you mean, mean what you say. It makes sense doesn't it? Less complicated.

When painting, dancing, or making music, go as deep as you can go – your real depths of passion, compassion and love. Connect with who you really are.

Create with repetition

Start with a repetitive motion, repetitive brush strokes, repetitive movements, repetitive rhythm, chord, repetitive note, phrase or chant. This will take you to a deep place.

Make some bad art

Try to make an ugly picture, ugly song, awful dance. You may find that this actually may take you to a new place you don't usually visit. It may open new doors – take you out of the box.

Opening vision to Oneness

Look with new eyes. Everything is alive: the chair, the trees, the instrument, your painting. You are connected by being in relationship. Everything has energy and is vibration. Notice the energy and vibration you share.

Trust painting

Make a painting with your eyes shut. You can do this with oil pastels or swirl colors of paint with your eyes closed. Ask to be guided. Open your eyes and look as if it were the first time you ever saw a painting.

Respect your art

Thank your picture, song, or dance. Approach it with wonderment. If you are having difficulty, repeat as a chant, "I accept myself, I love and accept myself."

Thank you

Spend a week giving gratitude. So grateful for all there is. Notice how the mind chatter stops when we come from love and gratitude.

Practice giving and receiving

Go to nature; receive its gifts, take away inspiration for your creations. Look at the textures, patterns, movements, sounds. Give back to her by singing to her, dancing to her, or creating a painting of her. This is an important exchange of gifts. Nature likes to be acknowledged as we do.

ALLOW

What feelings want to be expressed? Give them full expression. Do not censor. Make friends with what is going on with self.

TELL THE TRUTH

Honesty will steer you away from self-deception and avoidance. Depth and quality arises from resonating with inner truth. Truth empowers you. Are you willing to express authentically?

KEEP IT SIMPLE

There is depth in simplicity. There is more opportunity to go deep in your heart when the sound, art, or movements are simple. When our ideas are complicated, there is a tendency to play from the head. Play without effort; it is so simple. Breathe. When we are in the flow, creating is effortless.

When you find yourself getting into your thoughts, explore with repetition.

LET GO OF JUDGMENT

Let go of the need to be good. Allow yourself to make mistakes; they may be the doorway to a new perspective or discovery.

ONENESS

Separateness encourages comparison: Who is better? Breathe – this will connect you back to the infinite, the oneness.

TRUST

Trust that the Source is there for you. Trust the process. You already have everything you need. You might have just forgotten.

ACCEPTANCE

Accept your gifts. Have compassion for what you just created. If you want the muse to come and play, be gentle.

GRATITUDE

Be grateful for the gifts you received. Thank what you just created for manifesting. Thank the muse for coming to help.

GIVE AND RECEIVE

Discover the balance of giving and receiving. Give to the creator as you receive from the creator. Remain empty so you may receive the gift. Give the gift back to the creator through sound, color, movement.

How about sharing your gifts with others? Sometimes our works are for us, not to be shared. Check in with your body. What is it telling you? Does it want you to bring your work into the world or is it for your private healing? Many creative people have difficulty bringing their gifts to the world. The process of sharing our creations is similar to creating them. We learn many lessons in life and art in the process of sharing our gifts with humanity. When manifesting, there are cycles to the creative process.

Nine Cycles of the Creative Process

Making a painting, writing a song, writing a poem, or developing a dance piece is fun and rewarding – yet it also takes commitment, hard work. From our improvisations, one may fine-tune what has been given by spirit and develop it into a piece to be given back. This could be: write a book, record a song, develop a dance performance, a workshop, healing through arts, a community event. Your desires could be to develop a practice of self-discovery and empowerment through the arts. You might start a painting, write a song, or create a dance. I want you to be aware of the cycles of the creative process so your flow is not thwarted by a disappointment, of being blocked by our concept of time. Once you are aware of the process, you can recognize, "Oh yes, that is a stage in the cycle."

1. INSPIRATION
2. FEAR
3. INTENTION
4. PREPARATION
5. ACTION
6. WALL
7. INTEGRATION
8. BREAKTHROUGH
9. MANIFESTATION

These cycles are not linear; they may change order or repeat. The important thing is movement, or else nothing happens. Then there is a block. I will demonstrate the process through one of my experiences of creating community through the arts.

I moved to a new home in Phoenixville, Pennsylvania. At the time, this town had a stigma. It was an old steel town and the steel industry had fallen. Many of the stores were vacant; it was like a ghost town. In my travels to many beautiful places, I would wonder, What am I doing in Phoenixville? Community is very important to me, yet I could barely relate to most of the people in my town. I did not know anyone else interested in the arts, except my husband. My realization of why I was in Phoenixville began with an inspiration.

Stage 1: Inspiration: I had a vision to make a mosaic mural.

Stage 2: Intention: I wanted to make a large mural in town with the community.

Stage 3: Fear: I had some fear: "How am I going to do this? I never did this before."

Stage 4: Preparation: I realized I needed support. I wrote a grant and hired someone with experience to help.

Stage 5: Action: I solicited support from the community. I put up signs: "Who wants to be on the mural design team?" Eleven people showed up. At first I thought, "How wonderful." As we tried to work together, I thought, "Me and my big ideas. How could I expect eleven people to come up with one design?"

Stage 6: Wall: Well, I had given up control of the design by inviting these 11 others. It was not going the way I wanted.

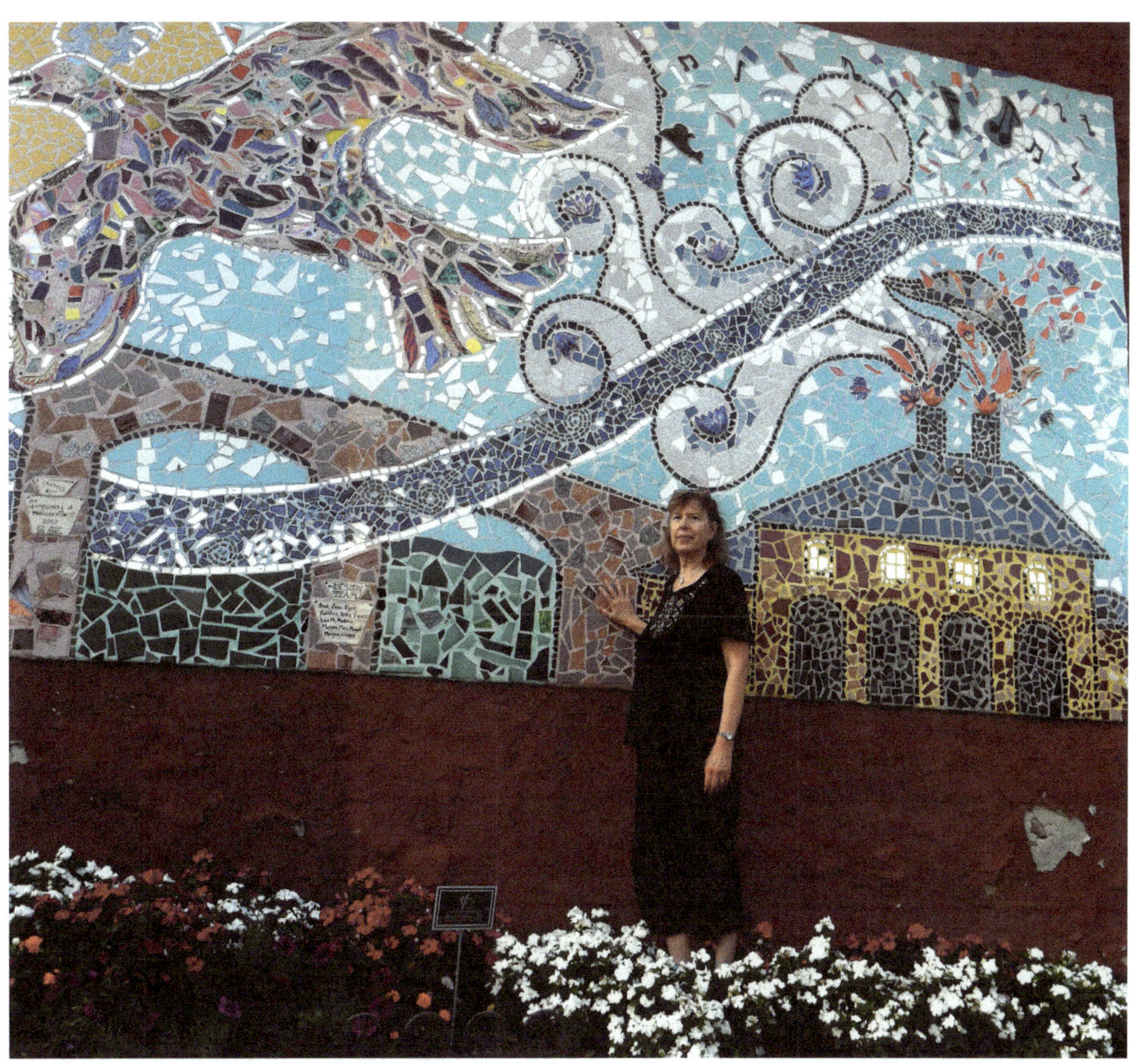

Phoenix mural, Lynn Miller and community. Photo Judy Robinson

Stage 7: Integration: I looked for new solutions even though it felt chaotic.

Stage 8: Breakthrough: I asked one person to create a design that incorporated everyone's design ideas.

Stage 6: Wall: I literally hit the wall again. I lost the wall the mural was going to be on; the building sold overnight. I had everything ready to go with community volunteers to help install the mosaic. I had a deadline to complete the grant or loose the money. The stress moved me to stage 2.

Stage 2: Fear: I became physically ill.

Stage 5: Action: This took me within on a self-healing journey.

Stage 7: Integration: Looked for new solutions.

Stage 8: Breakthrough: Someone came to me with a new wall. It ended up being better than the first – in a neighborhood that does not get much attention. The people felt proud.

These cycles wove in and out several times. The happy ending was I found a whole community of other artists who came out to help with this project. We have continued to be friends and have created other community arts projects together. The entire town has gone through a transformation, partially from our efforts. The town has become an arts community.

I have seen the wall come around enough that I realize the breakthrough is right behind it. I remind myself: This is part of the creative process; don't give up. I share this so you can identify the difficult parts as part of the cycle of growth.

Manifestation through Transformation

In order to live, you must be willing to die

Mother earth shows us how to live, die, and grow. Her cycles of the seasons mirror our experiences. Look at her movement to learn to be in the flow. Follow her rhythms to learn about creation. Life, death, and rebirth are the process of creation.

In order to set the stage for creation, it is advisable to slow down the doing and tune into being. Nature is a wonderful environment for receiving messages.

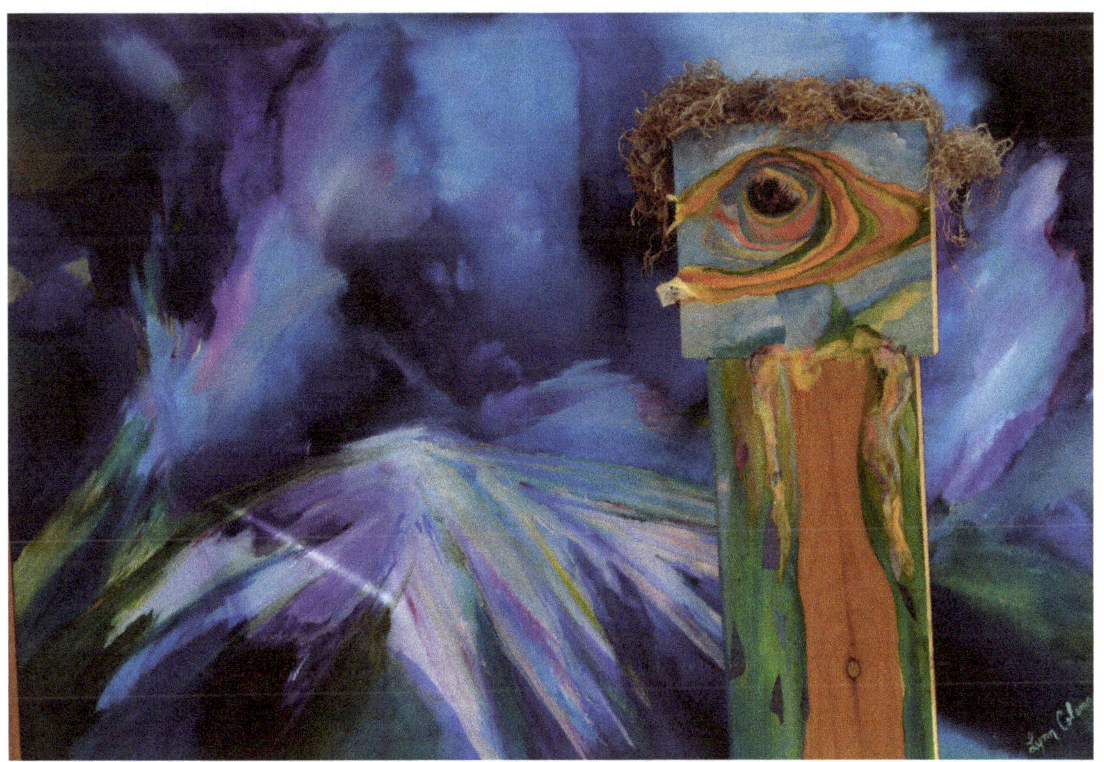

Inspiration, Lynn Miller - photo by Julie Weber

INSPIRATION

In this stage, you may feel an excitement or uneasiness. This is energy calling you toward an art form or project. Pay attention to this energy – you are being guided. If you don't listen, the energy will stop. The muse will throw you a bone. If you never catch it or persistently ignore the cue, they may go elsewhere. Look for the signs – you may have a dream, attraction, vision, feeling. You may not know exactly what it is; it may be a feeling at this stage.

Inspiration breath

Breathe in and out, inhale/exhale. With intention, breathe in inspiration, breathe out fear. Let the fear blow away with the out-breath. Breathe in inspiration, breathe out fear, breathe in inspiration, breathe out inspiration, breathe in inspiration, breathe out inspiration……..

LISTEN

OK, you heard the message. You may weigh out: How much energy will it cost me? Is the fear too large? Will the project take up too much of my energy? Do I not feel ready? Will it take too much time from my job or family? Will I lose money? Will I anger others? Will I need to change too much? Is it too uncomfortable? Many of these questions are taken into account. If it does not feel like the right time, if you do not feel ready to commit, the creative process ends or picks back up at a later time.

Have you ever met someone with a lot of ideas and desires who is not ready to commit or take the risk? Possibly it will cost them too much – to quit a job or whatever the individual feels is keeping them safe. Someone may fear poverty if they seek their dream. Our culture puts value on the material: Did you make money doing it? If not, why do it? Possibly one does not need to quit their job. If the dream is integrated into their life, they may enjoy their job more, looking at it as a means to support their creative endeavors. In other cases, your soul does need to leave certain conditions in order to create.

Dance with fear

Acknowledge your feelings by drawing, singing, moving, or dramatizing them This will help them to be acknowledged so movement can occur. Trust.

FEAR

You may have fear and want to deny that you can do this. Believe in your imagination; anything is possible. Know that you are not alone; your guides are co-creating with you. Notice your thoughts when your mind stuff is present. Go back to the 4-step process: breath, body awareness, heart, stillness, or deep listening.

Discern if you are withholding your dreams because of fear. When you withhold your dreams or gifts, you are withholding your energy. When you look at your life story, do you have any unfulfilled dreams? Something that you did not give attention to or you did not express because you did not want to rock the boat?

Our lives are art. Every moment you have choices. A choice to be safe, take a risk, live in sadness or joy. Sometimes it feels correct to withdraw – like nature goes into death in the winter.

Contract and expand

Lay on the floor: Contract your body, make it as small as you can. Crawl into a fetal position. Now slowly stretch your body expanding, opening like a star.

How did it feel? It feels good to expand and to contract. You just don't want to stay in one position all the time. Be mindful to practice the change of both to create balance.

As we have more experience facing our shadows and our fears, we may learn to go through the stages faster. The fear stage may last only minutes rather than weeks. The shadow may be faced quickly rather than stuck in it for years.

Grace, gracious, grateful – appreciate every moment no matter what the circumstances

Our ego thinks there is not enough – not good enough, do not know enough, not enough time, not enough talent.

Play to the end breath

You have two breaths. Take the first breath, sing until there is no more breath, almost to point of gasping for the next breath. Your body will naturally take in a big breath and sing to the end of this breath.

You may be surprised how much sound you get in two breaths. The second breath usually brings authenticity in the sound. You are enough!

INTENTION

You have awareness of what you want to express, such as opening up musically, wanting to paint, knowing you want to dance, create a CD, performance, etc. The clearer your intention, the easier for the muse to hear your message so it can co-create. Sometimes we are split with unclear messages – then the muse doesn't know what we want.

PREPARATION

You decided to follow through. You are percolating over the creative expression – getting ready. How might I do this? This is the time for gathering information, gathering materials, research, getting psyched, or possibly making changes toward a more creative environment. When you show the universe you are willing to do the work, take the risk and carry out your desires or inspiration given you; you will be given more inspiration. If you are not willing to take risks in order to stay in safety, your creative impulses will slow down or cease.

ACTION

This is follow-through. Show up and take the steps toward what is needed toward manifestation. Pick up the paintbrush, begin writing the poem, play the song.

But I don't have time to practice. Make practice a part of living. It is a practice to practice. Wherever you are, there are possibilities of practicing, even if you do not have your journal or guitar. This will help keep you in the discipline, even when you are away from your place of practice. There is music everywhere – listen to the birds, the wind, a pencil drop. Look at the shadows, blotches of light and dark when you look at a cluster of trees. Look at the textures in the tree bark. Move across the room mindfully. Shut your eyes. Imagine yourself moving. Imagine yourself in nature. Imagine music. What do you hear? Be grateful for the moment. This is all part of the practice of awareness. Make art life and life art. This will keep you in the flow when you are away from your creative endeavor.

Ok, You have acted on the desire. It is moving along steady and – what's that, a wall?

WALL

Things have become chaotic. Something difficult shows its face. This may be your shadow, (addressed in Section III). "I am not good enough." "What if they don't like it?" "Why did I even start this? It is too difficult." When you seek approval from another, you will most likely not receive the approval until you find it in yourself. You are giving power away when you seek their approval. Why do you seek their approval? Do they remind you of a parent figure or authority figure in your childhood? You may need to change negative programming with positive affirmations. "I love myself, I love the way I sound. I accept myself, I accept the way my painting looks."

There may be an internal block: "I don't have any ideas." "I feel blocked." Remember to make everyday a practice. Go back to your senses: take a walk in nature, ask for guidance, get out of your way.

There may be an external block: someone or something tries to stop the flow. Someone tells you, "No, you cannot do this." Or you lose your space, lost the funding, no one shows up or you are put down. The external wall is there to strengthen you. Now is the time to stay with your process without pressuring yourself or losing momentum of the intention, something will unfold at the right time.

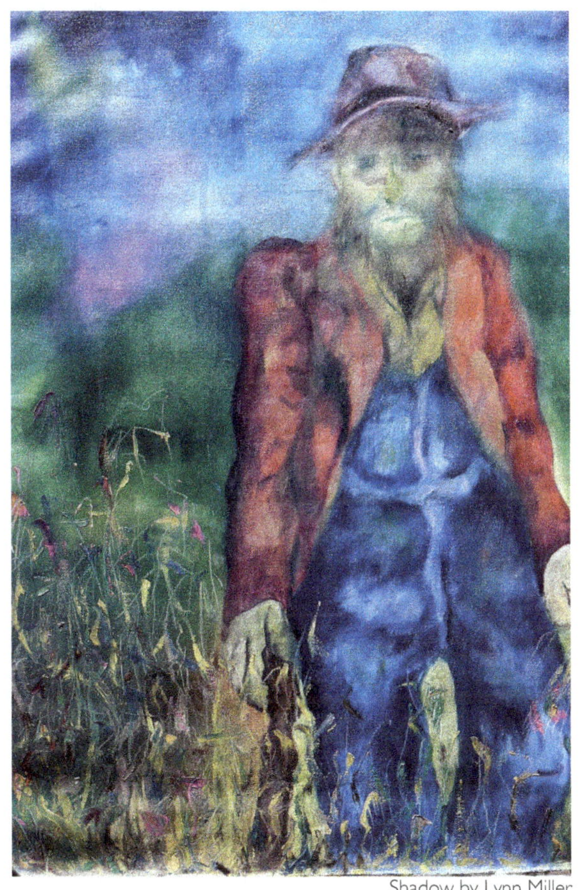
Shadow by Lynn Miller

INTEGRATION

Stay on the path; be persistent. In this stage, you integrate the shadow. Despite a disappointment, you look for solutions to get through the passage. The more the shadow is hidden, the larger the lessons of learning. The universe wants to know that you are serious. More opportunity.

Creativity comes alive in change. If we are stuck in any of the stages, there is less movement. There is no right or wrong; we simply are where we are. We have choices each moment to moment. We have a choice to change our perspective or attitude. Take your cues from your body. How is your body responding? Check in. What are you feeling? Is the body feeling contracted? Is it trying to tell you something? Is it giving you messages to change perspective, move through old beliefs or perceptions? Is there something we don't want to look at (denial)? The arts are a safe and effective way to help us change our perspective. Sometimes our images have something to tell us.

Give up attachment and control. Invite insight, be willing to understand the lessons and then accept what is.

OPPORTUNITY

Look at roadblocks and obstacles as opportunity. Something new is discovered after we hit the wall. You are being asked to confront the block, go deeper within. Go back to the 4-step process: breath, body connection, and connection with spirit. Listen for solutions.

Perspective Exercise

Create a drawing or painting. Turn it upside down. Look at it turned sideways. This changes the order, the balance. Maybe it wants to be upside down. Do you see new insights from the upside-down perspective?

BREAKTHROUGH

This is the Aha! Moment. Creativity comes through, new discoveries. You are in the flow. It is effortless. It is exciting. Everything is working. You are in a state of timelessness. It is blissful. There is a connection to the universe, new life, rebirth.

MANIFESTATION

Something was just birthed and the cycle continues for the next life/death creative process. You will see these cycles over and over again. If you identify a cycle as part of the creative process, you may move from one stage to the next in faster sequence. The stages do not always work in order. You may start with the wall and end in fear. You have met inspiration and you fear; you won't be able to do anything as good again. You will also notice these stages in your daily life for anything you wish to accomplish. Acknowledge that you are in a stage of the process, especially if the feelings are difficult. When things get hard, sometimes we cannot see our way out – we feel stuck. Trust the process; it is a cycle one must go through for deeper inner knowing. Once the cycle completes, it starts over again. One stage is not better than the next, even though one stage may feel more at ease. The cycles are like seasons – life, death, rebirth. Trust the process; they are all part of the process of discovering the jewels within. As we travel through the creative process, we meet our fears, our bliss, have a thousand lives and a thousand deaths. A new project is born; it grows into something and comes to an end. I hear a new whisper: Oh, a new inspiration…it's really all part of a cycle..

I have a fascination with the Phoenix myth. No accident I happen to live in Phoenixville. The Phoenix is a transformation story told in many cultures. The Phoenix is a magical bird that lived for thousands of years; it had the most beautiful song and most beautiful feathers. A time came when it was losing its vitality. It built a nest for its funeral pyre. The nest went up in flames. A worm grew out of the nest, creating a new Phoenix. This story tells the life, death, rebirth story.

I saw the parallels of this story in my town. Once a booming steel town, then a ghost town. I felt it important for the community to realize the power of this myth, so I helped create the Firebird Festival. The vision was to build a giant Phoenix sculpture in town, fill it with clay birds built by the community and light it on fire. The baby birds would be fired by the burning of the old. Sounds pretty far-fetched.

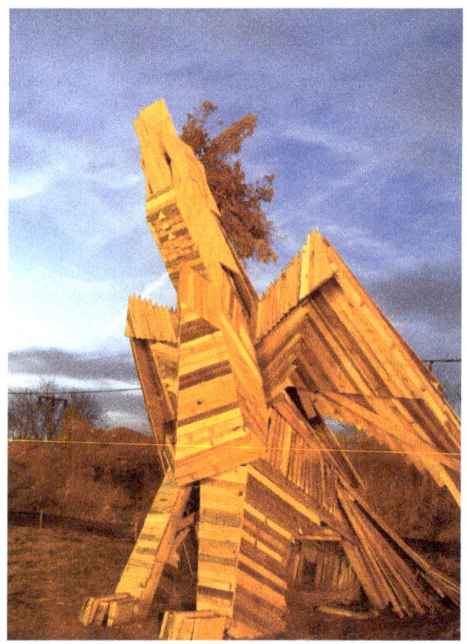

28' tall Phoenix sculpture.
Different sculpture every year

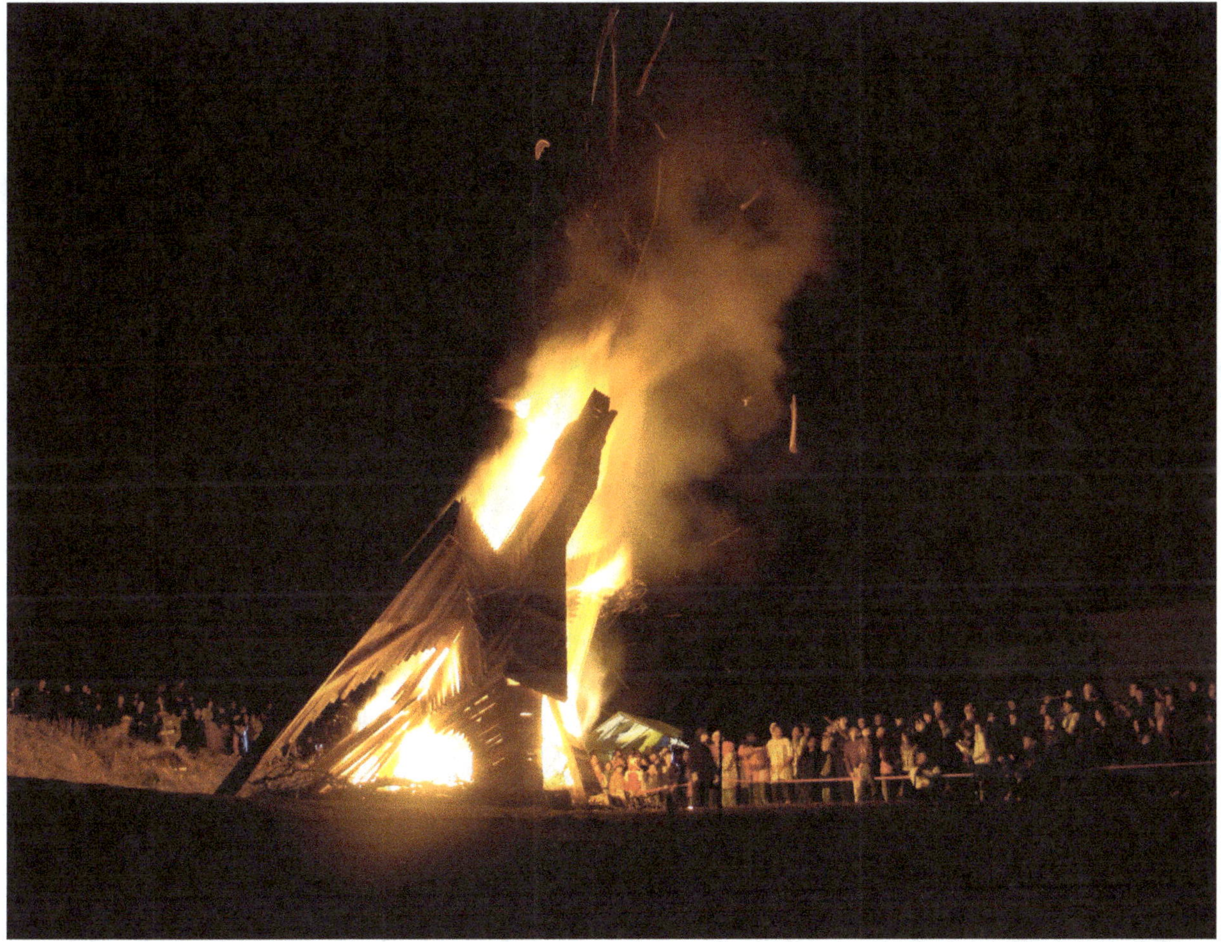

Burning Phoenix sculpture, photo by Henrik Stubbe Teglbjaerg

It has manifested. We now have a giant bonfire every winter, attracting thousands of people to this small town. The intention for this festival was to bring arts to the people and prosperity to the stores who were struggling at that time. Since our first bonfire in 2004, the town has gone through a transformation – attracting artists, restaurants, galleries, and community.

As you can imagine, not everyone thought it was a good idea to burn a giant Phoenix sculpture in town. The wall cycle was pretty big on this one. Through persistence, this festival has brought rebirth to our community. Over 16,000 people came to watch the sculpture burn at the most recent festival.

Persistence is important. The fruits will not flourish if the plants aren't watered. Sometimes we feel we have been watering the plants but the growth is so slow....

Is-ness chant

Close your eyes, chant 'Is" for a moment. Allow the ss-sounds like z z z to linger – your teeth coming together – makes something like a bee sound. Allow your neck to move with the vibration, unravel. It may move up and down like a wave or in circles. This may transport you into Universal time.

Time

Linear time, our clock time, works in the realm of cause and effect. It is a measurement device. Take this action and expect to get this response back within a certain time period. I have worked toward a project and known others who have worked very hard yet did not receive the energy back as fast as desired. This causes frustration. I have learned that my personal timing is not always the same as universal timing. My ego may feel it deserves manifestation now. Trust that if you keep showing up, the time is perfect. This may also mean showing up with being-ness – the dream, not always doing. Possibly the universe wants you to have more knowledge or your work needs the time to develop on a deeper level. The creator has a master plan.

On the other side of the coin, I have witnessed or experienced manifestation instantaneously. What one would call being at the right place at the right time. Creating in the moment goes beyond space and time. When open, some of the most amazing creations appear effortless and instantaneous. This is truly magical and synchronistic.

In the spiritual dimensions, there is no linear time as we know it. Universal time works in the present moment. All creation happens in the present moment. The present moment is all there is and ever will be. It is the moment to create. When we are in the flow of creating, there is no time. You may be surprised when you do look at the clock that you were there for five hours when you thought you were there for one hour.

The rhythm of your soul is more in sequence with Universal time. In Universal time, anything is possible. Dimensions come together; all there is exists in the moment. Everything just is. Is-ness. Everything is eternal.

Allow. You have shown up, asked for help or guidance, and feel you have not received the energy back. Time for some fine-tuning. The frequency of your desire must match the frequency of your being in order for it to resonate or attract you. You must be open to receive it, to allow it to flow to you.

Vibration

Everything is vibratory. Vibration exists in all things. We may look solid but we are made of vibrations. There is an energy charge with the vibration of every thought. Vibrations with like frequencies resonate or attract each other. What we think and what we say magnetizes a like frequency. It is important to be consciously aware of what we say and what we think. Being conscious will attract the higher vibratory gifts of life. Without form, all there would be is intention. Intention is the essence of creation. Be mindful of your intentions – what you say and what you think, for they are creation. Watch your intent: Are you focusing on what might go wrong or what might go right? When you approach your art with the energy of joy, that vibrational foundation will reciprocate. Only stay with what brings you joy. Joy is when you are in your power. Power comes through by telling the truth, what you really feel. Joy is when we feel connected to our feelings, connected to ourselves, to others and to the creator.

It is time to bring out the dreamer. Become clear on truly what you wish to do-

- Sing from the heart
- Play my own music without reading from a page
- Create a painting from the inside without copying from a photograph
- Dance my dance from my inner rhythm

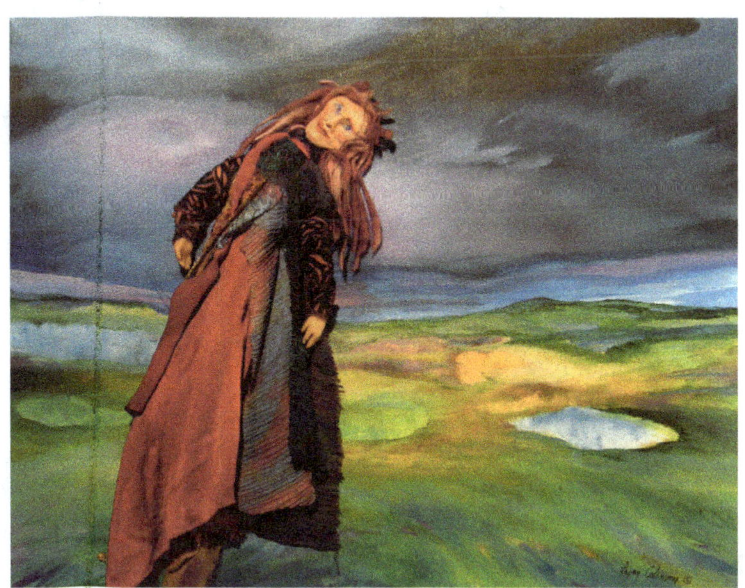

Doll and painting by Lynn Miller

Intention is part of the co-creating process. It is letting Spirit know what you want. Make your intention clear in the present tense such as, "My intention is to be open to the images that appear;" "My intention is to allow my voice to come through;" "My intention is to allow anything that can happen, to happen." The clarity of your intention will magnetize the manifestation of your heart's desire. What excites you? Interests you? What do you want to expand? It is time to take off the shackles imposed by your culture, family, teachers, and education system. Let the dreamer in you open to the possibilities.

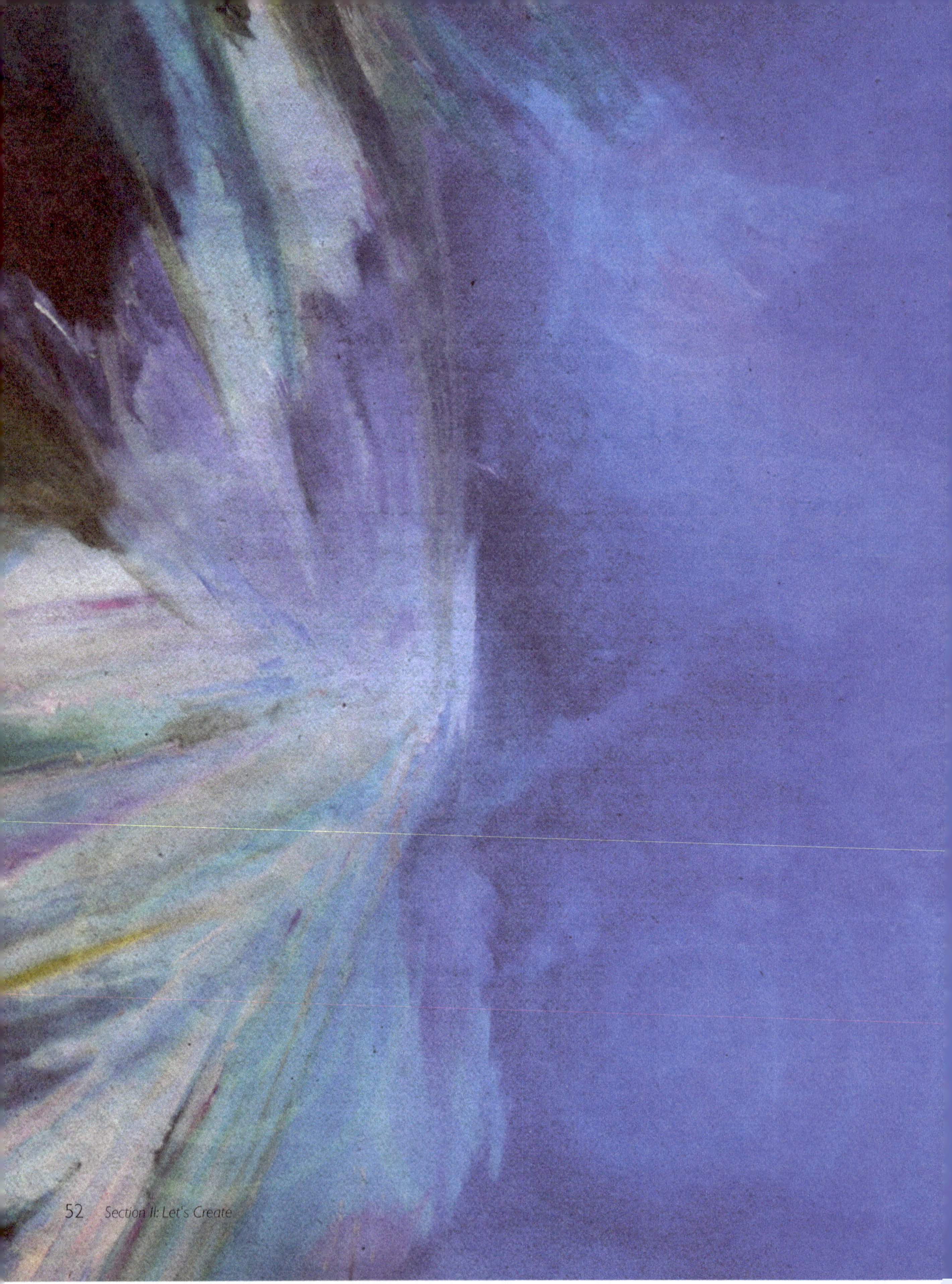

Section 2: Let's Create

It doesn't serve the world to hold back your creativity

Let's Create provides exercises in movement, music, and visual art. Pick the modality you are most drawn to or give yourself permission to explore them all. Once you have played in one modality, apply that experience to another.

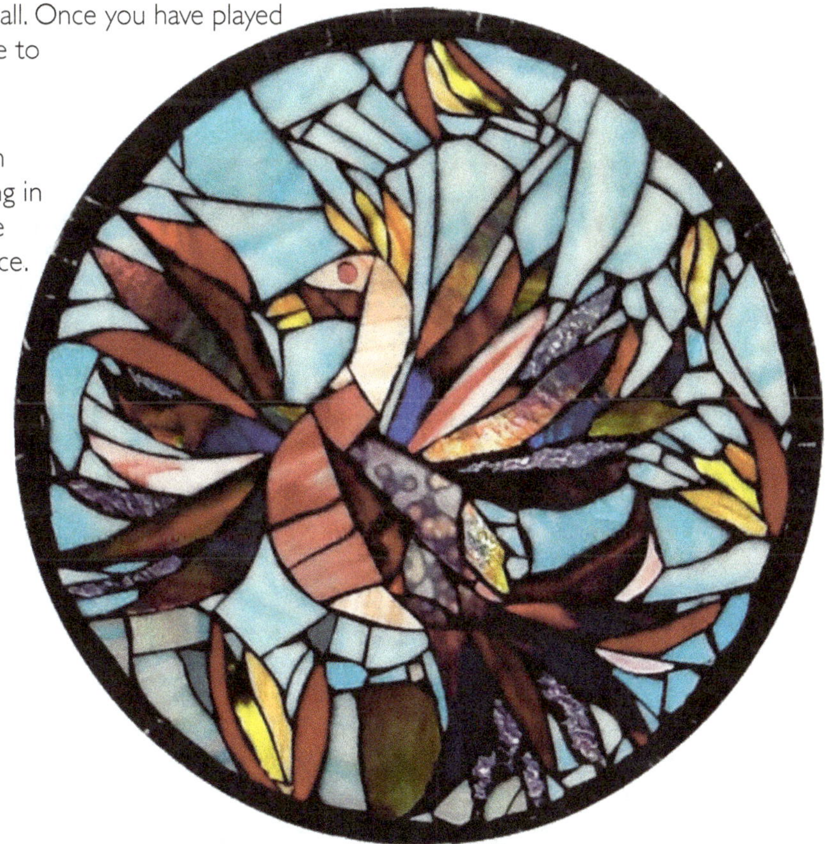

Phoenix stained glass, Lynn Miller

Explore each art modality by using an improvisational approach – by creating in the moment. Improvisation is possible for anyone, with or without experience. Improvisation is total involvement with creating. It is being present in body, emotions, mind, and spirit. Even though it is unplanned and spontaneous, improvisation is a practice. Practice the exercises in **Let's Create** to develop your artistry, express your soul, and develop your intuition.

Remember to approach each art form through the 4-step process:

1. Breath
2. Body
3. Opening heart
4. Deep listening

There is no right or wrong in improvisation. If the result isn't what you wanted or how you expected it to look or sound, you always have the next moment to refine it, embrace it, embellish it, accept it, or just stand in stillness and listen. If an exercise seems too advanced for your level of experience, skip it and come back after you have gained more practice.

The exercises range from very basic to advanced, so don't become discouraged. You could hang out with any one of these exercises for a lifetime, learning to master it. Practicing one exercise very deeply may be more helpful to you than doing the more advanced ones only intellectually, without learning to embody them.

If your focus is in art or dance or music, you may prefer to focus only on that section. These exercises have been compiled from years of experience, love for the arts, and the belief that we all can benefit from expressing ourselves through them. It all begins by accepting the risk of taking that first step!

These exercises are intended as a reference for you to come back to at different stages in your development. May they be your permanent guides toward creative freedom!

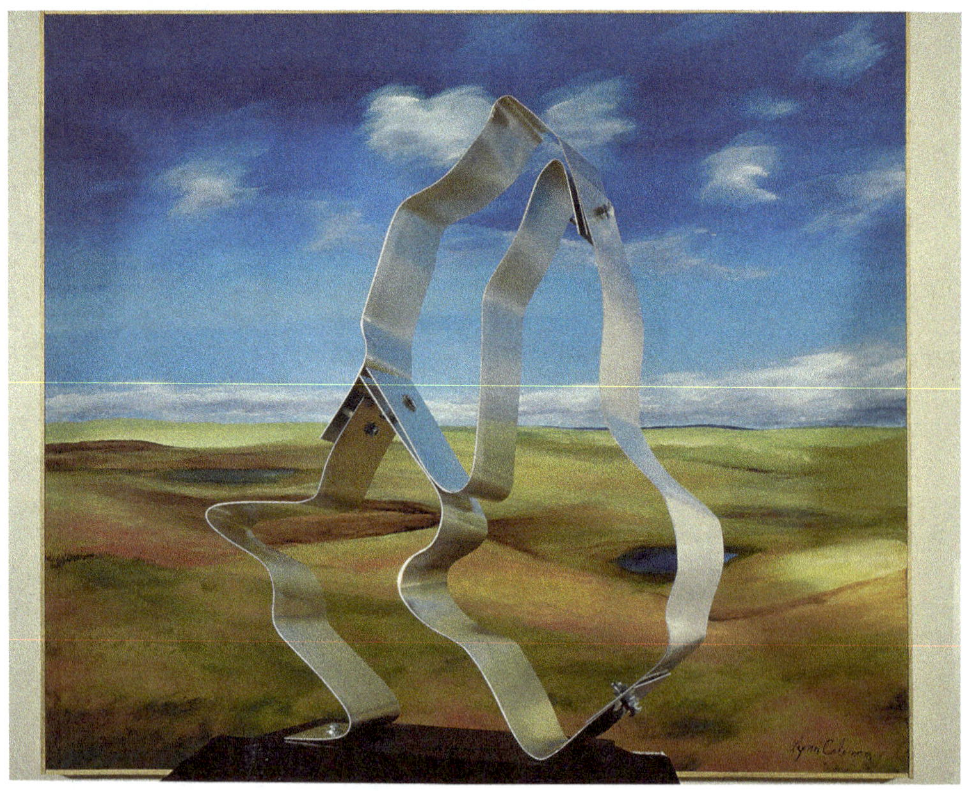

Sculpture Spike Coleman, painting Lynn Coleman Miller

The Spirit of Movement Improvisation

When we dance, we are dancing with spirit

> "We were born into an alien world in which the first movement was breathing – that sharp inflation of the lungs to bring the first cry" *(Whitehouse, as cited in Pallaro 1999, p. 33)*

As babies and toddlers, we communicated through our bodies before we had words. We learned through our bodies – touching and experiencing the world through our bodies.

As we grew older, we were conditioned by society to sit behind desks in order to learn. Learning became for the mind – a mind separated from the body. Many stopped learning through our bodies.

Exploring levels

Lie on the floor. Feel the ground. Begin from stillness. Move slowly from stillness. Breathe, let your breath and body guide such movements as - wiggle toes, move feet, roll legs, move arms and fingers. Roll to one side.

Slowly move to the middle level - crawling, crouching, or moving from knees.
Explore the middle level space.

Slowly move to standing. Explore moving in space - walk tiptoe, spin, skip, leap, jump.

Learning through body

Imagine learning through your body as if for the first time. How fascinating! Move your hands and arms; notice the energy in the space and the air. What does it feel like? Go up to an object such as a chair. Imitate what the chair looks like with your body. Become the chair. Now come into relationship with it. Move toward it. Move around it. Dance with the chair. Put your legs through its legs. Use it to balance as you stand. Make movements sitting on it.

Walkaround

In this group exercise, members walk around the room focusing on their feet on the ground and their crowns being lifted by a string. Dancers explore walking forward, sideways and backward.

The group begins to weave in and out.

Each dancer may change tempo, levels and add large and small movements or stillness. The group uses their peripheral vision to imitate others. The individual dancers may dance far apart or come together in close contact.

Relationship. When we move, we make relationships – relationship with space; relationship with the music, if we are moving to music; relationship with the ground, air, and gravity, if we are leaping; relationship with another, if we dance with someone.

Dance is an inner or an outer experience. Dance with your eyes closed. This takes you deep within your inner landscape. You might even voyage into awareness beyond yourself, into the vast unknown. Now dance with your eyes open – as if seeing for the first time. Open your awareness to the other, whether it be the room, objects, or people. Opening your peripheral vision is important when dancing, especially in a group dance. You will develop your intuitive sense when you practice being aware of everything and everyone around you. Practice dancing with your eyes slightly closed to balance your inner and outer awareness while dancing.

I have been exploring dance improvisation for more than 17 years with Kristen Bissenger at the Feet First Dance Studio. Before each class begins, Kristen prays on the class, listening for the theme or intention (deep listening) of the highest good for everyone involved to dance to. For example, she prayed on one class and heard "...teeth and tongue." She asked for more illumination on how to dance this and heard "...bound and free flow." The teeth represented bound and the tongue free flow.

Since spirit speaks symbolically, some deciphering of the answers we receive is often required. We danced the interplay of bound and free flow exercises, and ended with a free improvisation developed from previous explorations. Other themes for dances have included: trust; be at peace; release; truth.

We often begin class with a walkaround that develops our deep listening skills, tuning our inner and outer awareness. Kristen's sister, Cheryl Cutler, also teaches dance improvisation. Cheryl describes a walkaround in her book, Creative Listening (p. 59), along with ways to use dance improvisation to overcome fear in life and work.

Dance elements may be explored while doing the walkaround. There are many ways to begin an improvisation from a shape, an impulse, a contact, a repetitive movement, or stillness. Remember, when you move, you are connecting, making relationships with self and/or other.

Elements of dance...

Dynamics. Add dynamics to what you are in relationship with. When in relationship to the ground, collapse/rise; in relationship with space, move fast/slow; in relationship to music, bounce/vibrate; in relationship with the air, heavy/light. When in relationship with the other, you may contrast your movements with rigid/free flow.

Imitation. Imitation is a very powerful tool when dancing with others.

Variations. Imitate another by moving in unison. Now, make variations on their theme by making a similar movement but using a different body part, at a different level, in a different tempo, or with a different dynamic.

Repetition. Create a short movement theme. Stay with it; repeat it. Move to something else and then come back to the repetitive theme or movement. The repetition creates the ground that the other dancers will use to work from by mirroring or making variations on your theme.

Tempo. Move slowly, then repeat the movement in a faster tempo, create a new phrase, and change the rhythm.

Stillness. When dancing with a group or alone, adding stillness creates contrast and interest. It gives you the opportunity to tune in and listen deeply.

Shape. Begin from a shape: spherical, triangle, box. If you have a group, begin from a group shape. Think of positive and negative space (the space between you and other). This makes another shape. The shapes help to develop composition. Be aware of your shape, the group shape, the shape between the dancers, and the open spaces.

Sometimes we move a sketch, other times we move a composition. When moving a composition, as in music, dance has a rhythm or structuring of patterns, such as a beginning, middle, and end. You may start with a theme, develop it through contrast, variations, dynamics, tempo, repetition, until there is a resolution. Use your peripheral vision to notice your relationship to others. In the composition, use levels, dynamics, imitation, shapes, and stillness.

You could dance a lifetime by exploring just these elements of dance.

Move what you feel

Eyes closed, stand and connect with your breath. Bend your knees and feel your feet on the ground. Breathe and connect with how you feel right now. Make a gesture of this feeling. Repeat. After several repetitions, breathe and repeat the movement slower, then slower. Breathe. Did your feeling move or change? Move the gesture faster. Notice what you feel now. This process will help you be in touch with, deepen, or integrate your feelings.

Mirror Dance

Find a partner. One person is leader, the other follows. Move slowly so that the follower can match where the leader is going. Change roles of leader and follower. Come into synchronization so that you are both simultaneously leading and following. It is a fantastic feeling when you come into unison.

This exercise is called flocking (like geese) when done with a group. The leader is in front, and the group follows in triangle formation. When the direction changes, whoever is in front in the new direction becomes the leader.

Dance and music

Of course, dance has a great relationship to music. Music is an inspiration to dance and dance an inspiration to music. Find some music that moves you; or if you are lucky, dance to live music. Let the rhythms move you; let the rhythms loosen you; let the rhythms free you; let the rhythms be you.

Put on some music. Pick one instrument in the music. Let your feet or other body part imitate the rhythm of that instrument. Try moving to another instrument such as the bass or voice; now try the whole piece. Let your arms or other body parts express the feeling of the music; now let your whole body express the feeling of the music.

You can create your own music through vocal sounds and body percussion. Accompany yourself or have a partner accompany you. Try foot stomps, body slaps, clapping, playing the floor with your hands like a drum. If you are singing, explore vowel sounds, consonants, and words. Move close together to hear the sounds vibrate; now move apart and dance to those vibrations. Dance is a great way to communicate with another. It is also a profound way to communicate with yourself.

Inner Dance

Our bodies and our emotions are interconnected. How we feel emotionally is reflected in our bodies and how we move. It is beneficial to have an awareness of the body and to move one's feelings through the body. One can move anger, conflicts, blockage, and frustrations through the body with energy and motion. These feelings get moved out through the veins, muscles, and pores of the body, releasing and transforming the feelings.

Moving from Emotions

Dance from an emotion and move its contrast: happy/sad; cheerful/melancholic; angry/loving; nervous/calm; scared /brave; silly/serious/excited.

According to Expressive Arts Therapist Natalie Rogers, you can use several sources to move from (Rogers 1993, p. 54):

1. A feeling you have.
2. An image.
3. A concept.
4. A body impulse.

Moving from an image or imagery...

Create an image such as, "I am the wind that blows upon the sea." "I am a wave on the ocean." "I am a tree standing tall, weathering a storm." Images from nature are very inspiring. It is very much like dancing poetry. Find a poem that has a lot of imagery and dance the images, or make up your own images and phrases.

Taking inspiration from the images around us is great material for dance. Dance from the imagery of a painting. Look at its flow, rhythm, and colors. Become an image in the painting or the general movement of the painting.

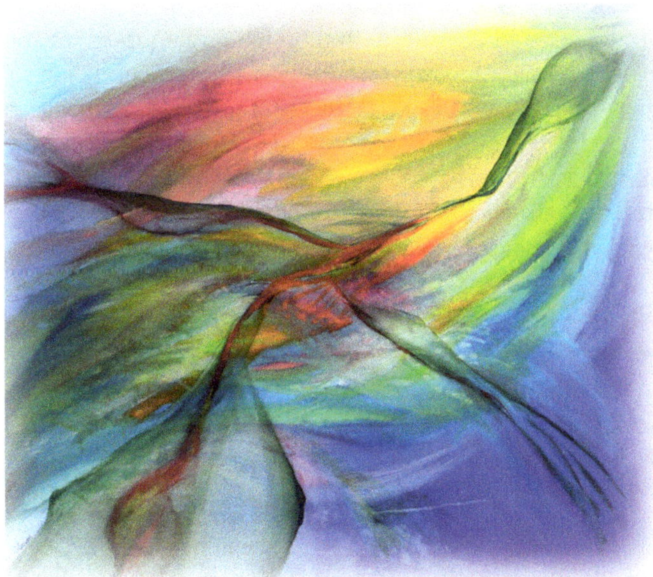

Spinal Painting by Lynn Miller

Let's dance as if we were a painting. Have paintbrush, paper, and paint available upon completion of this exercise.

You are the Painting

Imagine your feet as a paintbrush. Imagine dipping your foot into a color. What does this color feel like? What shape does this color want to make? Move your feet as the brush. How do you wish to apply the paint – squirt, dollop, dabble, scrub, opaque, transparent? Now move to the paints you had set up. Dip the brush in the paint color that attracts you. Move the brush on the paper like a dance. How does the color want to be moved – big strokes, smooth textures? Follow what the color wants to do. Move it as a dance. Move the paint as a dance.

Move the paint colors on the paper using your brush similar to how you used your imaginary brush, your feet. Did you find your painting had spontaneity, energy, and, of course, movement?

Move from your Emotions

Connect with your breath. Begin with an emotion. From this emotion, move into space. Dance with your emotion. Be your emotion. How do you feel: Awkward? Shameful? Embarrassed? Confident? Joyful? Free? Dance your feeling. Dance with shame or joy, then become it, fully embody it, let it move you. After you moved from one emotion, did you want to move from another?

Moving from a concept...

Dancing from a concept lets you try on the energy of moving into something that you would like to feel more of: "I am confident." "I am powerful." "I am strong."

Let's take an example of dancing power. To be authentic, begin from where you are. If you are feeling powerless, begin there. In the process of feeling powerless and allowing this part of you to be acknowledged, the concept may shift from feeling powerless to taking your power back. Or: Try the concept, "I am powerful." What does this concept look like? Feel like? Move it, embody it, become it. Make yourself BIG. Take up a lot of space. How does this feel?

Sue Mistretta, Expressive arts therapist, worked in a drug and alcohol rehabilitation center. She worked with some very big, tough guys. She helped them connect with their softer, feminine sides by putting on soft-colored lights, playing Vivaldi's ***Four Seasons***, and having them dance with colored scarves. Initially, they joked embarrassingly. But once they got into the rhythm of it, they went beyond their conditioned personalities. They danced with the feeling, "I am soft and gentle," as they moved in and out like goddesses in a circle dance. This movement helped them get in touch with a side of themselves they would not normally have shown or let out.

Women often need to connect with their masculine side, since many were taught to be nice and quiet. There was a time when I didn't want to make waves. I would go along with things out of my fear of confrontation. I suppressed my energy and my anger. Then I started to imitate martial arts moves such as chopping, slicing, kicking. Energetically, it translated as, "I am willing and able to protect myself." Once I felt this in my body, I was able to translate it to sticking up for myself in my life.

Fight for your empowerment or authentic self by chopping, slicing and kicking into the air. Let it out. Make sounds, yahhh! Protect yourself. Show you have the energy to stand up for yourself. Once we embody this part of ourselves, we will step out of the victim role. Energetically, others will respond accordingly.

Dancing the elements is another way to dance concepts:

Move the element of water - feel the flow, turbulence, stillness, reflections

Move the element of air - feel floating, breath, wind dynamics from stillness to hurricane

Move the element of earth - feel the ground, gravity, push and pull, support

Move the element of fire - feel smoldering, spark, igniting, energy

Moving from an impulse....

To move from an impulse, one must trust, let go, and surrender. The 4-step process – breath, body, opening the heart and deep listening – will prepare you to listen for the impulse. When you feel it, take the opportunity. When you feel the impulse, try not to censor or judge it – go with it.

Breath is the key to moving from impulse. Breath will let you sink back into your body, rather than moving from your thoughts.

When moving from a body impulse, you begin with no preconceived idea – you allow your body to be moved by an impulse. One impulse leads to the next: "Once your body surrenders to movement, your soul remembers to dance" (Roth 1997, p. 80). When dancing from an impulse, getting out of your own way and allowing yourself to be moved will connect you to your essence.

This is my story with dance and how I found the point of dancing from an impulse. I took tap dancing and ballet in kindergarten and loved to dance around the house, putting on performances for my family and their friends. As I grew older, I stopped dancing and became disconnected from my body – even ashamed of it. I suppressed most of my feelings. Feelings come through the body. By disconnecting from feelings, the body gets cut off.

Dance from your breath

Take a deep breath. Move freely to the end of this one breath. Take another breath and allow the breath to move you.

Dance from an impulse

Feet grounded, take a breath, wait for an impulse, and let the impulse move you. Let the impulse take you for a ride. Don't let it slip away; ride it if you feel it. If you do not feel it, keep breathing. The body is not stagnant – it will move, like water. The movement does not have to be big; it may be small and subtle. Small, subtle movements can be very profound on an inner journey.

My first husband, Spike, was a percussionist. He died at age 39. For his tribute, I invited his drummer friends to perform. That day, I told them that I wanted to dance with them. They were a group that drummed and danced together. At our first meeting, the lead drummer Bobbi said, "O.K. We want you to teach us how to dance." What? I didn't know how to dance. I thought, "You are supposed to teach me."

This experience became my reintroduction to being a dancer. I began to explore, teach, and learn – all at the same time. As a group, we taught one another. We studied each other's movements – we imitated the essence, the feeling, the attitude, the rhythm, and the shapes. I had to be clear in showing someone how I moved. It was my responsibility to show them. I learned to simplify so others could understand. We went into free movement after studying each other during our warm-ups.

The drums were an inspiration – the rhythms would lift me and move me. There was a letting go. My body did things I never could have thought or would have thought I could do. I would become full of energy even on days when I dragged myself up there, thinking "I am so tired. How can I dance?" When I moved my body, my feelings emerged. I learned to express these feelings, to let them out. I was able to get in touch with my grief and to move through it. Once your feelings are expressed and felt, a new energy and life comes to you. Dance is an extraordinary vehicle for inner and outer connection with the Divine, the self, and the other.

We have presented several ways to explore dance in the moment. What you experienced through dance can be applied toward developing your musical self. You will find overlapping similarities in the arts when you approach them improvisationally.

Spirit of Music Improvisation

My husband, Eric, and I are on the staff of ***Music For People***. The philosophy of the organization is that music is a natural creative expression available to everyone. Many of the exercises in this chapter and philosophies in this book were inspired by what I have learned through ***Music For People***. David Darling and my colleagues, Mary Knysh and Julie Weber, have also influenced the music philosophies I will share with you. ***Return to Child: Music For People's Guide to Improvising Music and Authentic Group Leadership***, compiled and written by Jim Oshinsky, has many exercises and structures for creating your own authentic music, as well as instructions on how to lead music improvisation groups. Grammy winning David Darling, the founder of ***Music For People***, developed the following ***A Bill of Musical Rights*** as a guide to help you express yourself authentically through music. David also created many of the exercises in the Instrumental music section, which we teach at ***Music for People***. They were developed from the core of how music works in many styles as well as from different cultures.

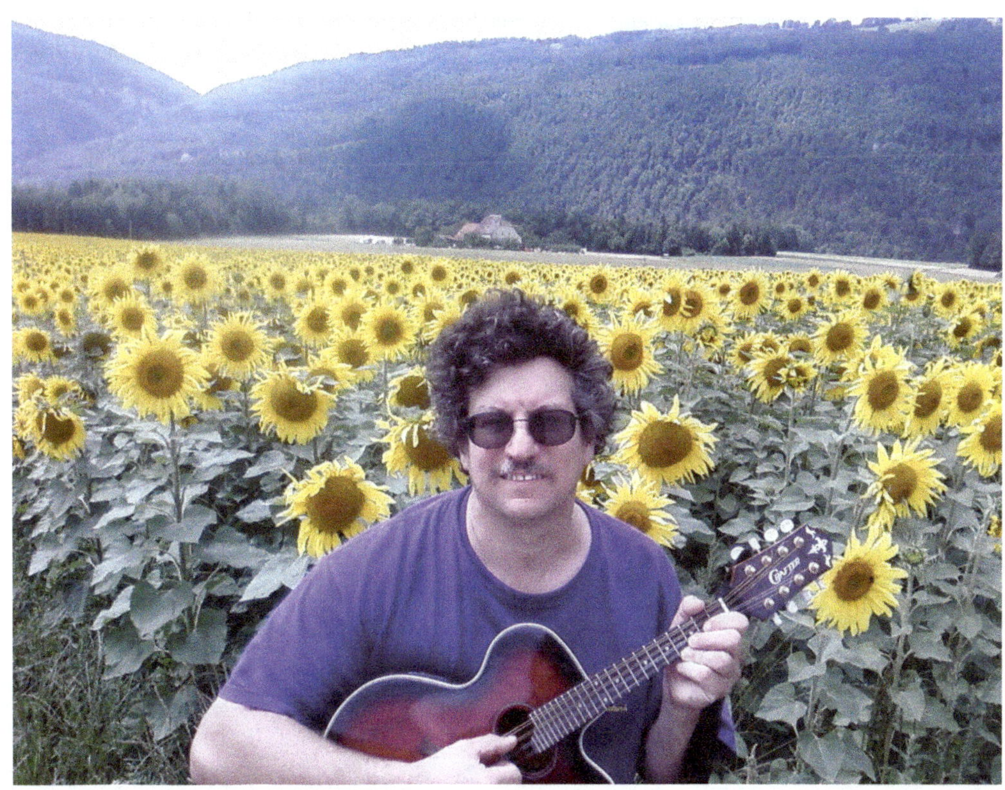

Eric Miller, Switzerland

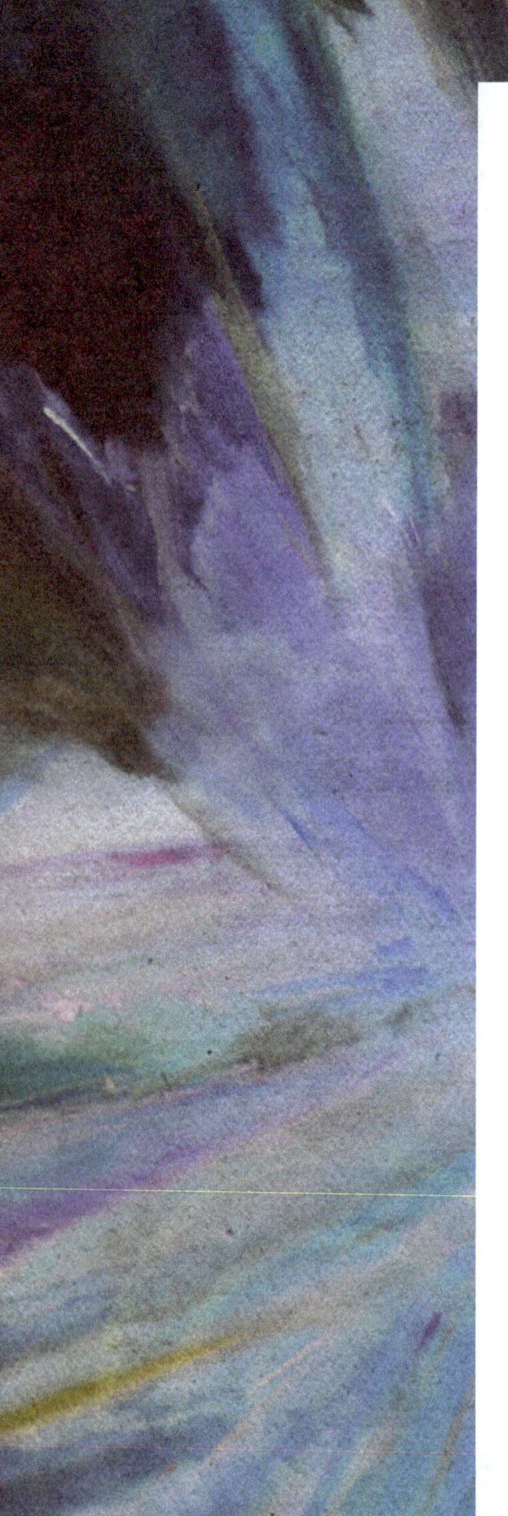

A Bill of Musical Rights

- Human beings need to express themselves daily in a way that invites physical and emotional release.
- Self-expression through music is a joyful and healthy means of communication available to every human being.
- There are as many different ways to make music as there are people.
- The human voice is the most natural and powerful vehicle for musical self-expression. The different tones of our voices add richness and depth to music.
- Musical self-expression begins with a genuinely-felt emotion.
- You will express your music more authentically if you involve your entire body in your musical expression.
- The European tradition of music is only one way of creating sound. The music of all cultures and traditions deserve equal attention.
- Any combination of people and instruments can make music together.
- There are no "unmusical" people, only those with no musical experience.
- Music improvisation is a unique and positive way to build other skills for life-expression.
- In improvisation as in life, we must be responsible for the vibrations we send to one another.

The following exercises can be used to enhance and deepen your own musicality. They can also be used to create music in ensembles with others – regardless of music style, instrument, or level of experience. These exercises can also be used therapeutically, when working with a group, to meet the participants where they are in the moment. At ***Music for People*** workshops, we create diverse ensembles by combining orchestra players with music novices, a dulcimer with a trombone, or a rock musician with a classically trained one. When creating music in the moment – improvisational music – we are all equal, involved together, listening to others' sounds while expressing our own.

Since the original musical instrument was the voice, the music improvisation section will begin with the voice. Many of the vocal structures described below can also be applied to most musical instruments. The exercises in the instrumental section can be applied to most instruments, including the voice. The exercises are beginning through advanced so focus on the ones that speak to you.

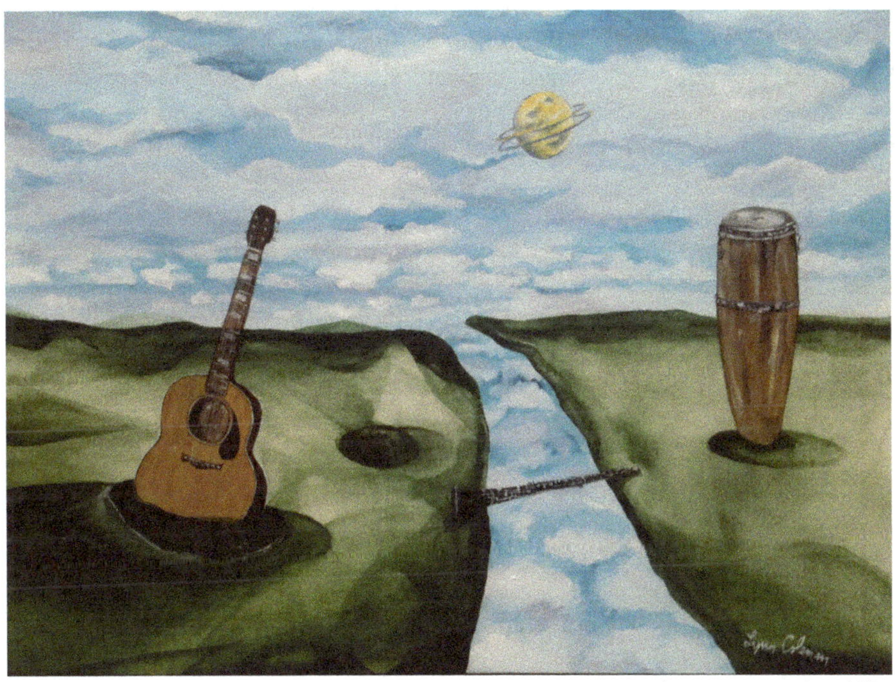

Instrumentscape, Lynn Miller

Exploring the Voice

Singing is a gift to express your soul

The beginning of the story for every person is that you first took a breath - and then a cry - as you came out of the womb. Sound was your first connection to the world outside of the womb. Even inside the womb, hearing is one of the first senses to develop. Our ears are a connection to the world outside of ourselves. Sound is the beginning of creation in many cultures: "In the beginning was the Word." According to Hale, the Keres people, the Athabasascan people, the Ancient Egyptians, and the Aborigines all have stories and myths about the world being sung into existence (***Hale*** 1995, p. 45). Sound is vibration; we are made from vibrations.

The voice is one of the most powerful instruments. We are gifted with our own built-in musical instrument that can be used for self-expression and healing. This instrument goes with us wherever we go and can be accessed anywhere, anytime. Your voice expresses who you are and what you feel. You can hear how someone is feeling emotionally and physically through their voice. Opera singer, Leontyne Price, exclaimed, "Singers are the object of the art, and singing is the most personal way to express art. It is you, you are it!" (Lewis 1998, p. 17).

The voice is such a powerful tool yet so many feel ashamed of their voices. As a music therapist, I have heard many stories: "The choir director told me not to sing: 'Just move your lips'." In my own life, I remember my dad yelling, "Shut up!" when I would practice my vocal range. These judgments often stay with us for life and can make us inclined to keep our mouths shut. Fortunately, I kept singing because it felt so good. Let's not give power to those judgments. It's time to open up and express!

The following exercises are ways to access you inner voice or authentic voice. We all have songs within, it is just most people have not had the opportunity to get in touch with them or a reference how to find them. The voice is a marvelous way to express these inner songs as it is the instrument of the body.

Warm-up using the 4-Step Process

The vocal cords that produce your voice are muscles that benefit from easy warm-ups. The 4-step process is perfect for this purpose; it focuses on diaphragmatic breathing and body awareness, encouraging you to stretch all of your muscles. The breath is the most important aspect to singing. The breath supports the voice. It also promotes relaxation. The more relaxed we are, the more the voice will flow.

When exploring the sounds of your voice and expanding your vocal vocabulary, it is all about how it feels: How does it feel in my body? Believe me, if it feels good, at ease in your body, it will probably sound good. If it feels strained, pushed, or controlled in your body, it will probably sound pushed and controlled. If you feel any strain, breathe and relax. Then go back to the 4-step process: breath- body- heart-deep listening.

Humming

Make gentle sounds with the mouth closed to warm up the vocal cords and body.

Sound vibration has been recorded as far as 3,000BC using the OM sound, the sound for universal vibration. Try repeating Om slowly with a long tone, breathing when you need to.

"The "OM" sound, as the ancient Hindu mystics learned, has an energizing effect on the brain and stimulates the pineal gland, which is the endocrine gland that rules the third eye (sixth chakra) and opens and magnifies intuitive ability." (*Garfield* 1990, p. 63).

Singing long tones helps to expand breath control, relax the mind and energize the body. Experiment with vowel sounds when singing long tones such as A, E, I, O, U.

Listening to Your Environment

The voice was the first instrument. Indigenous peoples and our early ancestors sang to the earth, the sun, the moon, and the stars. They sang to the creator. They imitated nature. The earth needs the sound vibrations of people singing, just as we need to hear the songs of birds.

Our voices are sacred and each one is individual. There are no two voices alike although some are pretty good at imitating others.

4-Step Process for singing

Breathe from the diaphragm. Notice what is going on in your body; stretch out muscles that need to stretch. Connect with your heart. Exaggerate and listen to the sound of your own breath. Allow gentle sounds with the out breath. Try low sounds and high sounds.

Exploring Humming

Make a humming sound. Feel it in your body. Move the pitch around. Notice where it vibrates. Where do you feel it in your body? Can you feel it in your feet, your belly, your chest, your head? Put your hands over your ears and hum. Feel the vibration, the depth, the infinite.

Vocal Exercises

Listening to Your Environment

Pay attention to the songs of the birds - they are for you. How do you feel when you listen to bird songs? Imitate the birds with your own voice.

What else do you hear? The wind? Make wind sounds.

Explore imitating the other sounds around you. We can all remember what a dog or cat sounds like. Imitate those sounds.

Meowwwww

This is a great vocal exercise. Sing: "MeeeeeeeeeOwwwhhhhhhhhh." Exaggerate this sound. When you sing the "ME," it places your voice in the proper position so that you will not hurt it. Can you feel the energy on the roof of your mouth and around your nose? This space is the resonator chamber for your voice. The vowel sound "EE" helps you go into your higher register and can open up the crown (energy slightly above your head).

High-Low

If you know what an octave is, sing the "MEE" in the high octave and the "OWHH" in the lower octave. (Alternatively, sing the "MEE" on a high note of your own range and the "OWHH" on a low note of your range.)

Now, go back and forth between the high note and the low note. "MEE" (high note), "OWH" (low note), "MEE,"" OWH." Feel the difference in how you make the two notes.

NOTE: What is an octave? Think of the Do-Re-Mi scale that we all know. The first "Do" is the low octave and the ending "Do" is the high octave: "Do-Re-Mi-Fa-Sol-La-Ti-Do."

Now put it all together: "Meowhh." Listen to the tone changes, and pay attention to what your mouth is doing. When you sing, think of it as playing with sound. Do I want to make a rounded sound like the "AHW" or a more pointed sound like the "EE"?

Mouth Cathedral

Now let's play with the "ohwhhh." Do this very slowly. What happens during this exercise is that your mouth creates a cavity. Think of this cavity as your cathedral. A beautiful high ceiling on the "OH" sounds like "AH." Now close on the "W," bringing your lips together with a small opening, just big enough for a straw to slip through. Do you hear the tone with your lips making a kiss gesture?

Vocal Range

The range of your voice is determined from the lowest note to the highest note that you can sing. Each person's range is different. Don't expect your range to match your friend's. You can explore the range of your voice with the following exercise.

Experiment with the siren exercise. As you slide up and down use your hand to follow the pitch-moving up or down. This gives a reference point where you are, enhances expression and helps connection in the body. Now as you siren, land on a pitch.

Do you ever sing in the shower? This is a great place to play with sound. It is important to listen to the sounds and be playful with them. When we become too serious we block the creative spirit.

Vocal Timbre

There are as many different-sounding voices as there are people. Different cultures also produce different vocal sounds and timbres. You may hear more nasal sounds in an Asian voice or with an American country singer or a Bulgarian singer. There is no vibrato (a small wobble in the sound) in those voices as there is in the European operatic voice. In India, they sing pure tones and the music scales contain all the microtones – the sounds in between the notes.

Exploring Timbre

Explore the diversity of sounds in your own voice:

Experiment with making nasal sounds. How does it feel? From this pointed nasal voice, begin to change the shape of your mouth. Changing the shape of your mouth changes the timbre of your voice. Can you add a vibrato?

Sing straight out, strongly.

Now sing softly, breathily.

Experiment with sliding your voice in small increments with notes very close to each other.

Sirening

Make a siren sound like a fire engine's - going up and down - as high and as low as you can go. This can be done with any sound. Wheee is a fun one!

Sliding

When you are in the shower, gently slide the sound "WHO" up and down your range, listening deeply. Do this close to the shower wall and listen for the reverberation. Stop when you come to a note where you hear the sound waves bounce off the wall. When you find it, stay there, chanting "WHO." This is a doorway into your power. Feel the many dimensions where your voice is taking you. Feel the reverberations bouncing on your body. Sing "WHO" from your heart, with the intention of sending love to yourself and the planet. That is true power.

You can also try this exercise standing up against the wall with your hands cupped around your ears.

Babbling, a Doorway to the Soul

We were all babies, and we all babbled. We were setting up our mouth and muscles for speech. Babies make the same sounds no matter what culture or language they originate from. Babbling is a universal language. Unfortunately, most of us forgot this language once we developed speech.

When we babble, it helps to loosen up all the mechanisms in our mouth to sing, just as when we were babies, it developed the muscles to prepare for language. Babble with fascination, as we did as babies. Wow, listen to those sounds! Babbling takes us out of our rational mind and right into our bodies. At ***Music for People*** we use it as a warm-up to "let go" of thoughts, judgment, honor the child within and get in the body. It is also fun!

Babbling is also a great warm-up before playing your instrument. Begin with the vocal babble. Move to your instrument and make babbling sounds with your instrument. This can take you "out of the box," widening your range of expression with little fear of "did I do it right?" There is no right way to babble. It is always different, out of our control. Babbling helps you let go……….

Yes, and how far can babbling take you? I propose that it can take you to your soul.

From Babble to Soul Language

By babbling, I am referring to non-verbal languaging. I will introduce several methods to access this special place within. The babble is an exploration of sound. When we get "in the sound," the sound takes us for a ride rather than us trying to drive it.

Let's try this exploration first with the vowel sounds. The vowel sounds carry the energy of spirit, carried by the breath. They are the sacred sounds. Now let's play with vowel sounds. Sing them slowly. A E I O U

There is power in simplicity. The long notes will center you. If you find your thoughts coming in, breathe, ground, sway your body and listen. Take it one note at a time and really listen. That note will lead you to the next.

Exploring Consonants

Consonants invoke the energy of matter, earth energy. When we ar-ti-cu-late them, we create rhythms. Try playing with consonants to open new worlds in your babbling vocabulary. There will be exploration exercises on the next page.

Try writing out combinations of vowels, consonants or combinations of the two and try to articulate them. This opens new ideas. Another approach is to sing without thinking, then write down the syllables you sang and learn your own language.

With wonderment, play with them as you might hear a baby fearlessly experimenting with new sounds. Develop your own rhythmic language. Now put your feet in the rhythm. Every time you make a sound, capture the rhythm with your foot or with clapping hands. This is a fun way to take a walk. It's even better if the birds join in.

Babbling Exercises

To Babble

Move your hands in a quick pulsing manner. Imitate this movement with your voice. For example: Ba-ba-la-ta-la-ma-ba ba la da Make up your own syllables. Whatever comes out is perfect.

With a partner, have a babbling conversation. Use your hands as you express one at a time to each other.

Babbling with vowel sounds

Feel your feet on the ground. Inhale with a big belly breath. Exhale long vocal tones with vowel sounds – AY, EE, I OH, UU. Pronounced AY as in say, EE as in free, I as in iee, OH as in low and U as in shoe. Notice how the mouth moves in different shapes with different vowel sounds. Play with the shapes. Listen to how the tones change. Repeat slowly. Mix the combination of the vowel sounds such as ie, ua, ui, iu, au, ei make up a little melody with your vowel combinations. Iou, uoi, aei, iea repeat and you have created a chant.

Add Y and H

Try adding a Y or H before or after the combination of vowel sounds.
For example: Ah a i /yo ee oh
Repeat and add a second part:
u ah u ah/ I e ah, ah ee, u ah yo

Babbling Consonants

Play with the sound of KKK, PPP, DDD, FFF, GGG. Feel how the consonants are made in different parts of your mouth and throat. Now combine consonants such as: KD-KD, FP-FP, GDK-GDK.

Combining Vowels and Consonants

Put a consonant before or after a vowel. Ka, Pa, Ma, Dig-a-duh-duh. Experiment with different combinations. Me Da. Da Me Fa. Fa. Ad Zee rahya kay gi di kah rah

Singing Your Name

Try combining both vowels and consonants through singing your name. First, slowly sing the vowels in your name. This is the sacred part of your name, from the heavens. Now sing the consonants in your name. This represents you on this earth. Now combine them. Play with different syllables and combinations in your name. These sounds can open new possibilities.

I have the opportunity to witness many voices in my work as a music therapist, educator and workshop leader. One aspect that never ceases to amaze me is the phenomenon of different voices we carry inside us. They are our soul voices. I love inviting participants to make up their own language-usually with a partner. People often giggle when they first do this exercise. I invite them to treat this as something sacred. It seizes to amaze me the soulful songs and interesting flavors of languages that come out. I am convinced we all carry these soul languages inside. Some may be afraid to open them up. Who are these voices and where are they coming from? I am convinced that these sacred soul languages are here to help us. The soul does not speak in a linear manner. It communicates symbolically. It is very freeing to finally let go of the ego and linear thinking. Once we let go, we are in the present moment, co-creating with the Divine.

Ga ta beta moon na key Na din
na pa reeta na Pa reeta di ney
Ha rey pa ta di na ra

Creating Soul Language

Feel your feet on the ground. Begin with a babble and start to articulate it. (Don't think) Use your arms with expression as you sing. Have this conversation with a partner, or if by yourself, converse with the cosmos. Example: Chi-ka ma yama day oh, day oh, me ayo. A partner may answer something like: Di shi kama, kama dishi dishi. You may find you begin to understand one another.

When you are singing, bring in your emotions. Connect in your heart area. Allow the sound to carry your story. The more you move, the more connected you will become. Move your arm and hand when you sing. Make the connection of the arm going up as you sing high and going down as you sing low. This will help you body map what the notes are doing. It will help you with your pitch-am I going higher or lower. Expressing with your arms and hands also helps to keep you from over thinking. Let the entire body express with the sound. Sing from your feet. Sing from your tail bone. Sing from your belly.

When you look in someone's eyes and sing a nonverbal language, you will see their soul. When you listen to what they are saying, you will hear their soul. Call your soul with a babble to remember this universal language.

I have the good fortune of working with a 7 year old girl whose mother brings her every week to remember her soul language. Her mother explained of the amazing languages she has created since 4yrs. old but was beginning to loose them after going to school. What an enlightened mother and child so full of wisdom. Her voice is remarkable with the soulful melodies and soul language she sings.

Dr. Zhi Gang Sha, author of ***Soul Wisdom,*** explains that soul language used with intention can be used for healing self, others and mother earth since it connects with the Divine and all souls. He feels there will be a day when soul language will become Universal communication for it comes from the clear part of our being and speaks to all souls.

It is my belief that all of us carry these ancient voices and languages inside. They are encoded in our cells. So, don't forget your daily babble. You will feel better. It may make more sense than anything else during your day.

Gisha ni gaia ah lay yana Dishina
ah re yah!

Spirit of Musical Instruments

Have you ever played a musical instrument? Do you have one sitting in the corner? Are you a trained musician who doesn't know how to play without music or doesn't know how to play with others? Have you always wanted to play an instrument but thought you had to know how to read music? Don't let that piano sit there like a piece of furniture. Pull out that trombone you played in high school; pull out that guitar. Has the piano been waiting patiently for you? (Remember, your voice is also an instrument).

Instrumental Warm-up

Begin with your breath. Then, warm up your body by stretching and moving spontaneously.

Move toward the instrument you know so well or are fascinated with. If you can pick it up, dance with it. Take a deep breath and play one note. Listen deeply to the sound. Repeat that note, or play another note. Continue one note at a time. Make each note so heartfelt that it leads to the next. Listen for the end.

Exploring Melody

When you approach music through your body, you bring your soul with you. When you listen to one note at a time, you are really listening to every sound that you play. To create an improvised melody, begin with one note or one quality sound. Listen to it. This will lead to the next quality sound, creating a line or phrase. Listening is the most important part of playing. When you approach music from your linear mind – which is how music education is often presented – you may forget to listen to your sound.

This is a great exercise to do with a group of friends or a musical ensemble. Stand in a circle or create a quartet with musical partners sitting across from one another. Breathe together, bring your arms up together as maestros and back down again while releasing the sound of one note. The game is for all members to come in with their individual note at the same time – not to try to match pitch with your partners. We call this exercise "One quality sound."

I have done this exercise many times at ***Music for People*** workshops and am always excited by the interesting harmonies created. Even if there is dissonance (such as notes being close together), there is magic in the sounds. Many cultures view power in the tension created through dissonance.

One Quality Sound

Take a breath and play or sing one note or pitch (just one!) until the end of the breath, focusing on listening to and loving your sound.

Develop a Melody

Let's go back to that one note you just played. Play it from your heart with conviction. Play it from how you feel right now. It could be loud and fiery, or soft and gentle. What is its emotional quality? Is it sad, happy, or melancholy? Convey the feeling of the note through air, force, tone, or texture. Now play another note. How does it sound next to the first note? Was it close or far away? Continue with another until you complete a phrase. Keep going, adding more notes and space in between the notes. You have just created a melody.

"One quality sound" teaches us to trust the unknown and to surrender into the moment, becoming one with the sound. As a group exercise, it connects the group – first by breathing together, then by coming in together. This can be a way to start an improvisation with an ensemble. The following principles may be applied toward the next step in a group improvisation, or in creating your own improvised melody.

Creating an Improvised Melody

Learn to honor all notes. Each one has its own personality, its own color next to another. Imagine there are no wrong notes or wrong sounds when improvising. Give respect to each note, even when it is a surprise or not what you were expecting.

Whether improvising from a scale, or starting from the unknown by randomly starting with a note and letting your intuition guide you, the following musical principles will assist you in creating your own music from the inside out.

Start with the 4-step process: breath, body, opening heart, deep listening. Begin from silence. When you feel the impulse, play one note with feeling, how you feel right now. Add another, feeling each note as you play it. When you tell your story authentically through music, both you and the listeners will believe you and find interest in what is being said.

Repetition

If you liked the phrase, play it again; this is your statement or theme. It will become home.

Creating Variations

Make variations on the phrase. Elaborate on it, turn it around, play it upside down. Play it backwards, add or delete notes in the phrase. Add notes close together or add leaps.

Form/ABA

Take a walk from home (or your musical theme) with different phrases, then come back home. This is telling a story. I started here, went over there, and came back to where I started. This creates a beginning, middle, and end – now you have a form. Jazz musicians call this an ABA form. The B part could be in contrast to the A part, it could be a stream of variations of the A, or it could be a new complementary group of phrases which leads back to home. Home is a repeat or a phrase or a feeling similar to your beginning statement.

Pitch Levels

Where did you begin your first phrase or note? Was it high, low, or in a mid-range? You have choices. You may stay in the same register or move up or down in range. Experiment with phrases that combine ascending and descending lines. Don't always start low and work your way up. That is a great form for building dynamics, but don't limit yourself – experiment.

Dynamics

Musical dynamics are the volume of the notes you make. Are the notes loud or soft?

You can create dynamics by playing louder and softer; playing the same phrase faster or slower; emphasizing certain notes. Stop and add silence. This really creates suspense. Stopping is also a great thing to do if you catch yourself not listening or not knowing what to do next.

Silence

Silence is your friend. When playing with yourself or others and you do not know what to play, stop. In an ensemble, silence creates interest with musical duo and trio conversations. Hold the space with your energy, take a breath, and wait for your next impulse or imitation of something you just heard. When you add silence to a musical phrase or melody, it creates interest in the composition.

Texture

Do not forget that texture can help you portray the emotion you are feeling. See what sounds you can make with your instrument. Animal sounds are a great way to experiment. You can also try imitating other instruments or the sounds around you. Approach your instrument as if you have never seen it before. What kind of sounds can you get from it? Try tapping on it or playing it percussively, like a percussion instrument. How about sliding, or making your sound shake with staccato, vibrato, or tremolo?

This technique can become very useful when playing in an ensemble and the instruments are not in pitch or tuned together. It can be a great opportunity to get out of the box and to find new, creative sounds in your instrument. Your intent is to make your instrument work, as if each note is your last one.

Embrace the Note

If the note you play is not what you hoped for or expected, avoid stopping to say, "Oops, I made a mistake." or "Darn it!" Embrace that note! It is calling for your attention. It may possibly lead you somewhere new – into new territory, a place you never thought of going. One approach is to restate that note or phrase as if you mean it and resolve it (probably right next door) or let it lead you on a new journey.

Remember, there are no wrong notes when improvising! If you open yourself to music from many cultures, you will hear sounds that your Western ear may say are wrong. In Africa, they play rhythmically from the heart, with less concern about tuning. In India and Bulgaria, they play notes that are very close to each other, seconds and minor seconds. To the Western ear, these may sound dissonant.

Do not be afraid of dissonance. It's a new world; get into it. Try to play a really terrible melody with all wrong notes. Playing this game will free the self from expectations and help you stay open to new sounds and ideas. You already babbled with your voice, now babble with your instrument. Have a babbling conversation with another instrument. It is fun!

Making melodies in ensemble playing

There is Power in Imitation

When you play in an ensemble and hear something you like, imitate it, double it, make variations on what you heard. This validates the other, shows that you are listening to others, and can give some glue to the piece. Call-and-response is a form of imitation: one calls and the other responds. Call-and-response began with the mother imitating her baby. It is one of the oldest forms of music. This imitative activity is used in many cultures and in the music of many religions.

Call-and-Response

The first person chants or plays a simple rhythmic phrase that is echoed back by another or by the group. In a group situation, this exercise gives everyone the opportunity to be a leader. It is supportive and empowering to hear your phrase repeated back. The call-and-response can be varied when the person answers with a variation on the theme. This variation can begin a musical conversation.

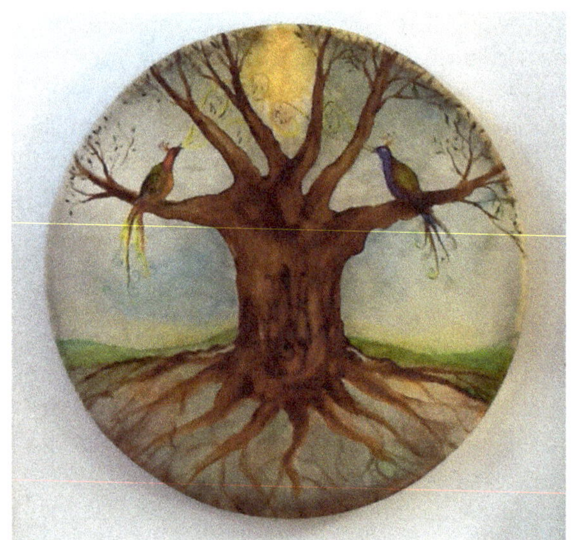

Bird drum, Lynn Miller

Shadowing

This exercise gives validation and connection with another. With a partner, one person is the leader and the other the follower. The follower mirrors exactly what is seen and heard, connecting with the essence of the other. Trade roles in following and leading, then find the special place of connection where you lead and follow together, or shall I say, no one leads or follows. Shadowing can be a great exercise in deep listening and developing intuition.

As the ***Bill of Musical Rights*** indicates, we all are capable of musical expression if we only give ourselves permission. We have explored ways to create a melody; now we will work on accompaniment. This could be accompanying yourself or playing with another.

Exploring musical accompaniment

Simple accompaniment leaves room for expansion

It is a great gift to offer an accompaniment for another. The following structures are easy ways to support self or fellow musicians. Many of these structures are simple. The simplicity offers freedom of expression for the soloist or melody maker.

Drone

A drone is one long tone. That is it: one long tone. You can do this! Try it with your voice: pick one pitch "ahhhhhhhh." Sing this while continuously breathing when you need to. Try it with an instrument. If you are on the piano, press the sustain pedal. If you are using a guitar or instrument that does not have a long sustain, you will need to tremolo the string or play the one note continuously for a sustained effect.

The drone is heard in music from many cultures: India, Ireland, Africa, and Scotland. The traditional drone instruments – the accordion, harmonium, shruti box, bagpipes, and illian pipes – make sound through the breath-bellows of a squeeze box. Bowed strings, such as with a cello or violin, can create a dramatic drone. This powerful, sustained note is home. It is safe; you know where it is; it's not going anywhere. This gives freedom to the soloist or the melody maker. Whether droning for yourself or another, it is a great support.

A Bulgarian singer told me that Bulgarian women sing when they work in the fields. Many pair up as both working and singing partners. One sings the drone, the other the melody. The drone is always the drone. She loves being the drone, the support. The singing partners are life partners, similar to geese with only one partner. She described that if one of the singers dies or moves away, it is very difficult to resonate with another partner. The singers are life partners.

The drone can be played as long, sustained notes, or pulsed, producing the rhythmic feel often heard in Irish music. For some instruments you may add a second note, such as a 5th, to make your drone. A second note creates an interval – the distance between two notes. Play the "do re mi" scale we all know so well. "Do" is "one." Then play five notes up the scale; do re mi fa sol. "Sol" note is the 5th note. Play "do" and "sol" together as one sustained pitch. Different intervals create different moods. "Do sol" is the standard healing interval, the perfect 5th.

In some cultures, the drone may change pitch to harmonize with the melody; in others, it never moves. When playing a single note or unison drone or adding a 5th or 4th, the soloist can play in either major or minor, or jump back and forth. It does not matter if you do not have a musical background or understand the difference between major and minor. Just play and experience the sound by how it feels in your body.

Drone in 5th's

Create a 5th on the piano, guitar, or other chordal instrument, or practice singing a 5th against a note on your instrument or with another singer. Experiment with long, sustained notes. Now try it rhythmically by pulsing the drone.

Solo/drone

Find a friend. One person creates a short melody: one quality sound after another, ending with a sustained pitch or drone. Your musical partner creates a melody over that drone. Switch back and forth, with one playing the drone as the other creates a melody.

Solo/drone chord

This exercise can be done with a group, with each one holding a sustained pitch after playing their solo. The sustained notes can be in unison or different pitches, creating a droned chord. After your solo, move to a different sustained note, which will change the chord.

This is a great musical bed for someone to create a melody. When developing a melody, experiment with the principles suggested in ***Creating an Improvised Melody.*** Try singing or playing notes that are close together (the in-between notes that you hear in Indian music). The drone supports the soloist for total freedom; anything you do will work. Try something melodic, dissonant, textural, or using a lot of space.

Play a drone. Play a sustained pitch on an instrument while singing a melody, or sing a drone while playing a melody with your instrument. You can also do this with a musical partner or an ensemble.

Soloing over two chords

This is the ultimate gift you can give someone: play two chords, such as Am to E7; hey, every once in a while add a third chord, if you like - like Dm. If you both know how to play chords, switch back and forth, with one playing the chords and the other the melody. Experiment with the suggested variations on a melody, presented at the beginning of this chapter.

Variations on the chords

If you know how to play extended chords such as 9th's or 11th's, you can open up the sound. If you know how to play chord inversions using these two chords, you will make it sound like much more than two chords. If you have no idea what I am talking about, check out Edley's ***Music Theory for Practical People*** to learn more. This book explains how music works. It is helpful but not necessary for improvising. You can create from just your gut intuition and your ear.

Creating chords by ear

A chord is more than one note played together. It is fun to make up chords, especially on the piano or guitar. You don't have to know what the name of the chord is. Play it from your ear, what you like. For an example, lay your hands on the piano keys with the fingers of your right hand spread apart.

Play all these notes at the same time. Now arpeggiate them by playing one note at a time. Change the accents or rhythms of the single notes. Hold them all down at the same time again, to create a chord.

Variations

On the piano, place your left hand on the bass notes, arpeggiate "151" - remember, "do sol do." Make block chord patterns by laying the fingers of your right hand anywhere. If you do not like the way it sounds, adjust a finger or two until you like the sound.

Continue playing 151 with your left hand while experimenting with moving the block pattern around with your right hand.

To make a variation on this theme, move the "do sol do" of your left hand to some other notes, while holding down a single chord with your right hand. Listen to what happens. Have fun playing with these changes. Don't think - just play with the sounds.

Ostinato

A repeated pattern is called an ostinato. There is power in repetition. Repetition creates the ground, the building blocks on which to expand. What a gift to one player if another plays a repeated pattern on a percussive or tonal instrument. This repeated pattern gives the soloist total freedom to build upon.

Try to create a three-note rhythmical pattern, such as "ga da goon," with your voice or instrument, and keep repeating this pattern. It requires focus to learn how to hold a pattern. Our culture is full of busyness. We may think we need to do more, but doing less allows more room for expansion.

Solo/Ostinato

One person comes in at a time with a repeated rhythmical pattern. It is best to keep the phrase simple, with two or three repeated notes using space. The space allows each voice to be heard. Once the parts lock in and a groove is established, the first person who began the ostinato takes a solo (or melodic phrase) while the others hold the repeated pattern. Eye contact is important with this exercise, so that it is clear who will take the next solo. After soloing, a new ostinato may begin as the next person solos. Try doing solo/ostinato first with voice, then repeat the exercise with instruments.

Exploring Rhythms

Listen for the pulse.

Play a heartbeat rhythm on a drum or your instrument.

> **thump** /thump **thump/** thump
> **thump/**thump

Feel the pulse. Listen for the "one." The "one" tells us where we are. And **one,** two, three, four, five, six, seven, eight...and **one,** two, three, four, five, six, seven, eight, etc. In all music, listen for the **one** – especially if you get lost. It will tell you where you are. Feel it in the body, where is the one?

Play with the pulse by changing accents, and create a new feel.

Clap with your hands:

> thump/thump thump/thump
> thump/thump
>
> thump/thump thump thump
> thump/thump thump thump

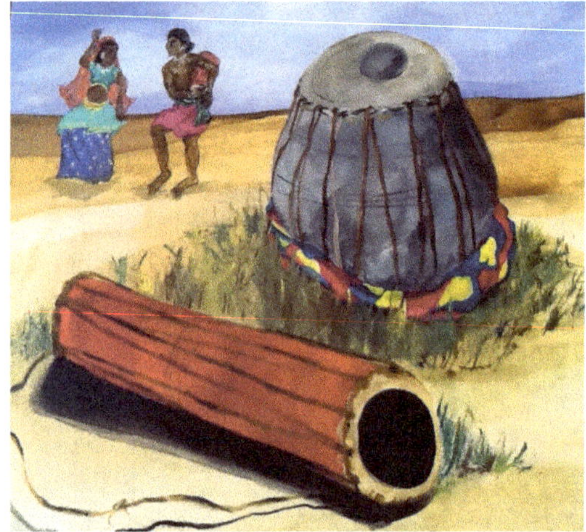

Tabla dance, Lynn Miller

Rhythm sets the pulse and "feel" of the music. Rhythm helps to define the style or flavor of the music.

You can explore the flavors of different cultures' music through rhythm. Our Western ear is very accustomed to music in 4/4 rhythm. More complex rhythms, such as in fives and sevens, are often very difficult for us to get the timing – our ears are not accustomed to them. Avoid traditional counting, since doing so can put you in your head. Best to feel the rhythm in your body. Many non-Western cultures use drum languages to teach songs and rhythms. They say it, sing it, move it, then play it.

Drum language

Below are patterns of drum languages from different cultures. Try singing them and moving to them. Put your feet to them. Then try playing them on a drum or instrument with a single note or chord. Sing them, dance them, play them. Practice repeating each pattern until you feel it in your body.

Any of these patterns can be translated using any instrument. If you are playing a drum, the "dum," "doon," or "ta" (depending on the culture) is the bass tone played in the middle of the drum. The other tones are played near the rim. The languages are imitations of the sounds that the different types of drum make. For instance, the Middle Eastern language imitates the doumbek, African the djembe, and Indian the tabla.

One could seriously study any of these rhythmic patterns for a lifetime. Which culture, drum language, or flavor do you connect with? Any of these rhythmic flavors can become ingredients for your own improvisation recipe. Many of these resources were compiled by Mary Knysh, author of ***Innovative Drum Circles.***

Middle Eastern:

Dum tak kah

2's- Dum tak

3's- Dum tak kah

4's- Dum dum tak kah

5's- Dum tak kah dum tak

6's- Dum tak kah dum tak kah

7's- Dum tak kah dum tak kah dum

African:

Olatunji from Nigeria was instrumental in introducing African drumming to the West. He created a method of teaching from the sounds of the Djembe.

BaBa Olatunji

Goon Doon Go Da Pa Ta

2's- Pa ta

3's- Goon pa ta

4's- Goon Doon go pa

5's- Pa Ta PA Ta Goon

6's- Goon-pa ta Doon pa ta

7's- Goon Doon go do pa ta goon

Rhythmic play

Combine any of the rhythmic phrases. Combine 2's with 3's, or 3's with 6's, etc.

Dum tak Dum tak kah Dum tak kah (rest) Dum tak kah dum tak kah

Make a phrase, then say it backwards

Dum tak kah dum tak kah kah tak dum kah tak dum

Dum dum tak kah kah tak dum dum

Drum language ostinato

Build a drum language ostinato. Each player comes in with a different repeated pattern on voice or instrument, such as:

Repeat Pa ta Pa ta. Next person repeats Goon pa ta. Next repeats Pa ta Goon.

Play with different combinations of these patterns. Once you develop a groove, trade solos. You can do these patterns with drums, melodic instruments, or voice.

Exploring Accents

Change the accents on any of the patterns. For example,

TA ki ta TA ki (accents on the 1st and 4th beats)

Ta KI ta ta KI (accents on the 2nd and 5th beats)

Ta ki TA ta ki (accent on the 3rd beat)

Drum language conversation

Sing your drum language, then imitate it rhythmically on your instrument.

Have a musical conversation through drum language vocally or with instruments.

TA ki ta ta ki da? **Someone answers:** *Ta ki ta TA ki TA ki*

Add melodic inflections, with the notes going up or down

Goon Doon go do pa ta goon? **Someone answers:** *Goon-pa ta Doon pa ta*

Rhythmic accompaniment

Play a repeated drum language pattern while another adds a melody.

South Indian:

Ta ka di mi

2's- Ta ka

3's- Ta ki ta

4's- Ta ka di mi

5's- Ta ka ti ta ki

6's- Ta ki ta ta ki ta

7's- Ta ki ta ta ki ta ki

You can make up your own rhythmic language in English - or shall I say ***Italian***-English. This is a fun way to learn new meters in a non-threatening, food-centered way. We all like food. If you are working with a group, you could ask each participant: ***What do you like to eat?*** Then make a rhythm game from the answer. Using the rhythmic language of Italian food may be an easier way for you to make complex rhythms simple:

2's- piz-za

3's- Spa-ghet-ti

4's- Ri-ga-to-ni

5's- meat-ball-spa-ghet-ti

6's- Ri-ga-to-ni-meat-ball

7's- Sau-sage-spa-get-ti-meat-ball

Use your imagination to open new worlds through rhythmic language. Have a conversation.

Exploring Scales

You can improvise with scales over a drone, ostinato, chord progression, or multi-cultural rhythms.

First learn the scale. To improvise using the scale, change the order of the notes in the scale. Create phrases using the same principles used in ***Creating an Improvised Melody,*** such as dynamics, repetition, variations on the theme, and adding silence. Don't forget to tell a story from your heart - possibly with a beginning, middle, and end.

The Pentatonic scale

This a very useful scale, since it is found in many styles of music – rock, folk, oriental, and blues. It is a five-note scale. Simply play all the black notes on a piano. Listen to the sound – that is the pentatonic scale.

The major and minor pentatonic scales are the most common in Western music. The examples below are in the key of C. (You must transpose to change the scales in other keys).

Major pentatonic - remove the 4th and 7th notes from the major scale:

1 2 3 5 6 8
C D E G A C

Minor Pentatonic - flat the 3rd and 7th notes and remove the 2nd and 6th notes from the major scale:

1 b3 4 5 b7 8
C Eb F G Bb C

The Blues scale

The blues scale is created by adding a "blue note" (b5) to the minor pentatonic scale:

1 b3 4 b5 5 b7 8
C Eb F Gb G Bb C

The blues scale is obviously very helpful in playing the blues. It is all about the feel, the phrasing, the spaces between the notes. Embellish the feel with slides, muting, hammer on, or pulling the note if you are using a stringed instrument.

Modes

Modes originated over two thousand years ago in Ancient Greece and were later used in the music of the Catholic Church. Many styles of music use them today. Each mode has its own flavor. An easy way to play the modes is to play all white keys, starting on C and playing to C (Ionian scale) The Dorian would be all white keys D to D-continue up the scale: Experiment with the sound by playing a 1 and 5 drone with your left hand in the key of each drone.

Below are examples of seven modes. For the Ionian, you play a C and G drone. For the Dorian, play a D and A drone.

Ionian	C	D	E	F	G	A	B	C
Dorian	D	E	F	G	A	B	C	D
Phrygian	E	F	G	A	B	C	D	E
Lydian	F	G	A	B	C	D	E	F
Mixolydian	G	A	B	C	D	E	F	G
Aeolian	A	B	C	D	E	F	G	A
Locrian	B	C	D	E	F	G	A	B

The Ionian is the same as the major scale.

The Dorian is minor, and is used in many jazz songs.

The Phrygian has a Spanish, Hebrew, and Gypsy sound.

The Lydian has a mysterious, flat 4th sound.

The Mixolydian has a flat 7th, and is used in rock, blues, and jazz.

The Aeolian is the same as a natural minor scale, heard in folk, classical and Irish sounds.

The Locrian has an unusual sound, and is not heard as often as the other modes.

Exotic Scales

Try out some of these flavors to add to your musical palette. They work especially nicely over a drone or a rhythmic pattern. If you are in the key of C, make your drone a sustained C and G.

Oriental:	C	Db	E	F	Gb	A	Bb	C
Hindu:	C	D	E	F	G	Ab	Bb	C
Arabian:	C	D	E	F	Gb	Ab	Bb	C
Balinese:	C	Db	Eb	G	Ab	C		
Gypsy:	C	Db	E	F	G	Ab	B	C
Spanish:	C	Db	E	F	G	Ab	Bb	C
Egyptian:	C	D	F	G	Bb	C		

Exploring Free Improvisation

All of the suggested structures mentioned below are to provide you more freedom to improvise with. Don't throw away anything you already know about music. Maybe you were classically trained. Use that knowledge and technique when you improvise. Then bring in your ear and your heart.

Practicing improvisation structures develops your ear and intuition for free improvisation. The following considerations will help in a free improvisation with an ensemble.

- Some instruments in the ensemble will be naturally louder than others. Make sure you can hear the softest instrument in the ensemble.
- Silence is golden. If someone steps out, yet continues to hold the energy, it will create duets or trios within the ensemble.
- Repetition is good. Whether the repetition is a drone, repeated pattern, or repeated melody, it will act as a glue for the composition.
- Create connection by imitating something you heard.
- Smile and have fun!

Whether improvising in-the-moment music by yourself or with others, the 4-step process is your doorway into the music: breath - body - opening heart - deep listening.

When we are connected in our bodies through movement, open in our hearing through music, and in our vision through visual art, we are more fully realized on this earth. It is time now to open your vision. You will find that the elements in approaching visual art without preconceived ideas are similar to those in creating music and movement in the moment.

Spirit of Visual Art

Open your vision and express your inner images

Most of us are visually oriented. Before we could speak, we thought in images. We constantly use our eyes to perceive the world around us. Our visual world is a reference point. It shows us where we are located physically in our outer world. What happens when we close our eyes? What do you see? Another dimension – our inner world, like our dream world. We all go to this inner visual place every night, whether we remember it or not. We have the ability to see inner visions – the past, the future. Many have cut off this natural ability because of fear of their imagery. Those symbols exist to help us, not hurt us. The soul speaks symbolically through images. We have many images stored within us. Creating art is a way of expressing these images.

> Everyone has a unique creative inner landscape of personal themes and images, a specific way of seeing and painting, of imaging and rendering as individual as one's fingerprint (Gold 1998, p. 31).

We will explore your unique way of expressing yourself through creating from your outer world and your inner world. The first set of exercises, **Drawing on the Outer World**, develops your ability to see your outer material world. These drawing exercises will help you to learn how to look and will stimulate your vision. Once you learn to open your eyes, you avoid illusions and find pleasure in what is around you.

The techniques in drawing what you see around you can also be used when you are drawing from within. They are two distinct ways to approach art: one imitates what you see before you, with possibilities of making variations on that theme; the other expresses what is inside you through drawing.

The second set of exercises, **Drawing on the Inner World**, focuses on opening your imagination and on painting from the inside out. Through ***Spirit Painting***, your intuitive self comes alive with awareness from the unconscious and messages from the soul. The soul speaks in symbols. Once the images come alive through visual expression, you can communicate with them, since every image brings a gift.

Visual expression can be articulated through many types of materials. Several types of media will be presented for your exploration. Each different material has its own unique personality and expressive quality.

Drawing on the Outer World

The outer world, meaning the physical world you see in everyday life, is full of inspiration. If you are ever unsure how to get started making art, just do a study of what is around you. Let's explore several ways to look and draw what you see. The following exercises provide several perspectives on creating form by drawing or painting on a two-dimensional surface like paper.

Materials: You will need a pencil, paper, and a flower or other object to study. Use a new piece of paper for each exercise.

Energy awareness

Find a flower or other object of your choice. Every object has energy. Check it out. Feel it in you. Rub your hands together. Slowly pull your hands apart, then close together, back and forth – then move them close together and pull them farther apart. Can you feel a pull, similar to pulling taffy? You are doing the QiGong exercise of creating an energy ball, a Chi ball. The more you practice creating the energy ball, the more you will feel it. Look at the flower or object of your choice. Look at it. Really look at it. Feel its essence. Take in the shapes, colors, textures. Feel its energy. Think of the succulence inside it; feel the energy of its colors. How does it make you feel? Move your hands close without touching it; then touch it and study its shapes and textures.

Shape

Look at the shape of the object.

Now notice everything around the object. Is it on a table, in a vase? Draw an outline of everything around it. Look at the different shapes you created.

Shadow drawing

With a bright light shining from behind you, or in bright sunlight, look for a shadow. Draw the shadow. It could be the shadow of your hand, a tree branch, or other object. Draw only the shape of the shadow, then fill in the space where it is dark. It will often mirror the shape of your object upside down, depending on the position of the light.

Drawing out the energy

Focus on the energy of the object. Without lifting your pencil, draw its energy. Move your body as you do this. Make a squiggle dance with your pencil, creating form through energy.

Line drawing

Make a line drawing of the object - an outline of its shape. The line will define what the object is, such as a chair, a tree, or a bowl, but it will appear flat.

Creating form. Make a drawing while looking at an object like an apple by using line and shadow. Incorporating shadow with the light will create the element of depth, giving your object a third dimension. The light with the dark creates a form.

Negative space. What is next to your object? Focus on the space between your object and what it is next to. If it is sitting alone, put it next to something. Draw the in-between space, or negative space. Look at the different shapes this creates.

Shadow. Begin a new drawing of your object, focusing on its shadow. Draw from the side of your pencil using different amounts of pressure - pressing harder or lighter. This will help create different shades of shadow. Look at the contrast. Where are the shadows darker and where are they lighter? Draw an outline defining the object, then fill in its shadow to create its depth and form.

Eyes closed. Look at the object. With a new piece of paper, close your eyes and draw what you saw.

Non-dominant hand. Draw the item with your non-dominant hand - the hand you do not write or eat with.

Variation. Create a new drawing, making a variation of the object you see. Make it larger, change its shape, color, or form.

Look at your drawings

What was your experience with the different ways of approaching the drawing? Some become fascinated with shadow and light, while others prefer simple outline drawings, capturing the essence of the object with the least amount of detail or just its energy. What was it like drawing with your eyes closed or drawing with your non-dominant hand? We don't expect as much from ourselves this way, which can be freeing. Did you find it freeing or confining to create a variation on the form? All of these exercises develop your awareness in seeing.

Composition

At any moment, you have the opportunity to look at your surrounding environment as a big picture landscape or to focus on its details by zeroing in on a specific object. Look around your environment and take in the big picture, noticing its shape and form. Now focus with great attention on something that is close to you.

Creating a composition

Composition is how things relate to each other in a drawing. When you create a composition, be aware of where you are in space. Think of a landscape: Is there a foreground with a more distant background or is it more open like space? Is there a focal point or main object in it? Where is that object placed on the page? What is its relationship to other objects? The negative space – the space between the objects – is also part of the composition. Possibly there is no focal point and the composition is open, with no horizon line.

Are the textures, lines, and shadows hard- or soft-edged? Is it balanced, symmetrical, or asymmetrical? Turn your picture upside down. Do the shapes look balanced? What is the rhythm of the piece? How does it make you feel? Art embodies the same elements as music and dance to consider in a composition:

dynamics • imitation • repetition • rhythm
silence • texture • form

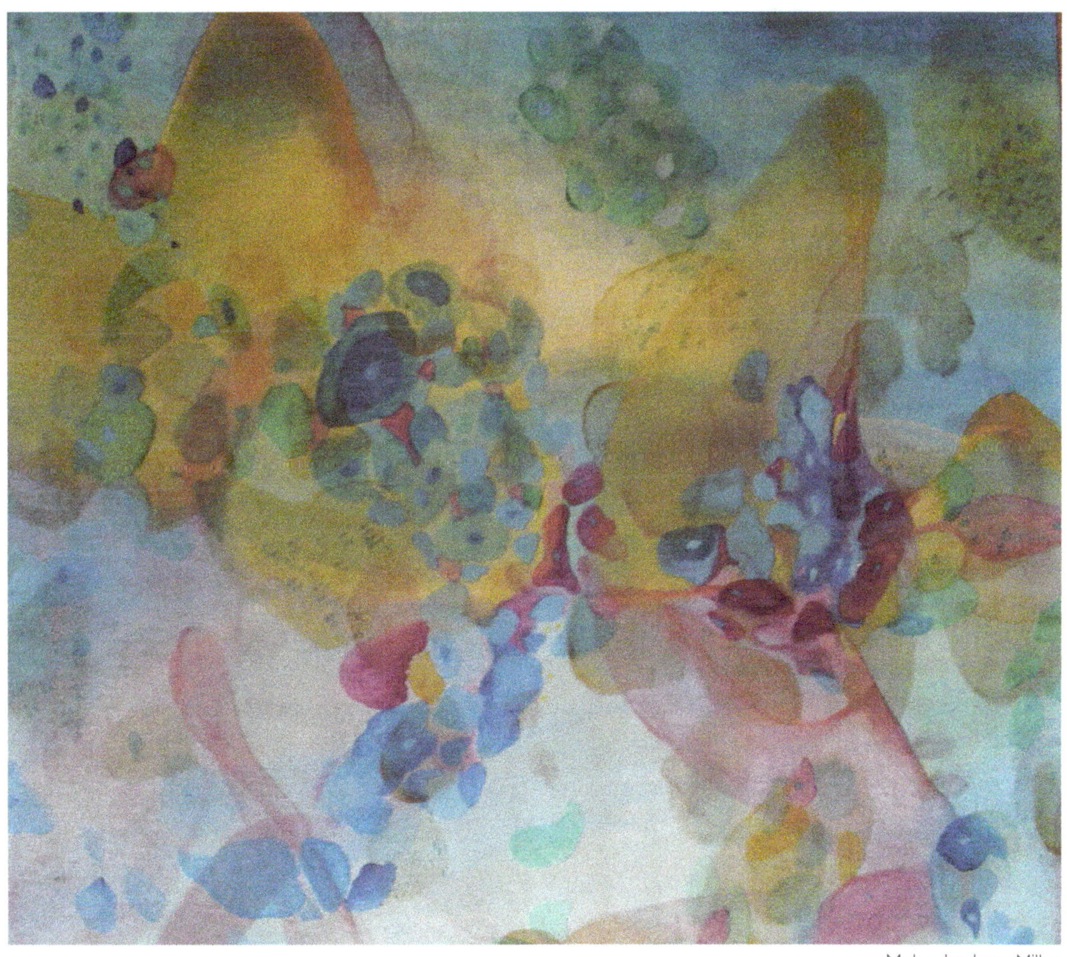

Molecules, Lynn Miller

Drawing on the Inner World

When we were children, most of us intuitively knew how to create visually. As our language skills developed, many of us stopped communicating visually. We learned to doubt our abilities to express ourselves visually; many of us became disconnected from this intuitive language. You may have forgotten how to paint intuitively, as you did as a child, but your body remembers.

Approach intuitive painting through the 4-step process, just as you did with movement and music – through breath, body, opening heart and deep listening.

Painting materials: *Poster board or other heavyweight paper. Acrylic or tempera paint in primary colors: red, blue, yellow, white and black. Additional optional colors: alizarin crimson, phthalo blue and yellow ochre. When you add water to these colors, they become very transparent. When you add white, they become opaque and provide many gradations and variations.*

Brushes: small, fine-point for detail, medium-sized and large for washes. They can be either acrylic or watercolor brushes.

Use a heavy paper plate as your paint palette. Remember, you can create colors by mixing the primary colors, or you can buy colors that attract you directly, by the tube. To mix colors, use a palette knife or your brush.

Painting tips

Formulas for mixing primary colors:

GREEN = blue + yellow

ORANGE = red + yellow

PURPLE = red + blue

If you add more yellow to your green, you will get a lime green; add more blue to get a forest green. You only need a little bit of each color. Put white in the middle of your the palette to add to your colors as needed. If you have leftover paint after you have finished, cover it with plastic wrap. If it dries slightly, add a little water.

Have paper towels or rags on hand and a large cup of water. When you change from one color to another while painting, first dip your brush into the water to remove the color, then dry it with your rag – this will prevent your colors from becoming muddy. Change the water if it begins to look muddy.

Experiment with water: use a lot of water for a transparent look or a little if you like your colors more opaque. Water-based paints will dry quickly unless you use a lot of water or paint. Once the painting is dry, you can paint over it to bring out certain details or to expand it into something new.

You may choose to listen to music while you are painting. It can loosen you up or put you in a trance state, depending on the music you choose. Music will influence the outcome, depending on its style – rhythmic and energetic, or slow and meditative. You may choose to paint from silence. Silence will help you to listen to what the painting wants but music can help you be in the body.

Spirit Painting

You may connect with an image in your minds eye or feeling in the body. Bring your body into the painting experience, connect with your breath, and move or sway. To start painting, choose a large brush. Notice which colors are asking for your attention. Begin with these colors. Apply them like a dance, physically using your whole arm, your whole body. Let the colors, not your mind, create the painting. Let them guide you toward what the painting needs. Continue to connect with your breathing – it will connect you to your body, feelings, the present moment, and the creative spirit. Connect with the mystery, the unknowing. Something will appear.

Once your paper is covered with paint, look at the colors and shapes to see if something or someone is asking to make an appearance. Do you see animals, objects, nature scenes or figures? Help to bring out this formation by adding details with a smaller brush. If you see no forms, perhaps the painting wants to express feelings and emotions. Bring them out through textures, colors and shapes. Feel the soul of the image through color and shape and honor it.

How do you know when the painting is finished? Listen for the end. How does your body feel when you look at it? Does it feel "antsy" or unresolved, or does it feel complete, with an ease in the breath?

If you feel that your painting is not complete, Aviva Gold, author of ***Painting from the Source,*** has some great tips for staying with your painting.

> **Paint faster.** Pretend that you plan to burn the painting. This will help you to stay in the body. Approaching the painting as if you plan to burn it helps you let go of attachment. Sometimes you will have an attachment for it to look good, or a certain way. Do not be afraid to let images surface or be afraid that you will "mess up."

> **Switch between large and small brushes.** Painting with the large brush helps you paint from your body. If you sit and plan and get your mind too involved in the beginning, you may get bogged down. Use the small brush later on to bring in the planning and detail part of the brain. Balance the two by switching brushes back and forth.

Switch dominant and non-dominant hands. Doing this will also balance the left and right sides of your brain. Painting from the non-dominant can move you into something you may never have thought of.

Switch between viewing close and from far away. Doing this will help to change your perspective. Also, turn the paper to look at it from different directions.

Paint with your fingers. This physical touch is especially beneficial if you find yourself getting stuck or worried. It will take you right out of your head and back to your body.

With Spirit Painting it is the process that matters more than the product. Accept where you are in the process. There are no mistakes, if paint drips go with the drip. When you look at your painting observe without judgment. Let the 4-part process help you paint from your heart, rather than the head. If you find yourself in judgment, go back to the breath.

Painting is a wonderful medium for going within because it is fluid. Moving the paint stimulates the emotions. Your inner imagery can be accessed in any medium. Each material brings its own gifts. Cater to the image. Does it want to be expressed as a two-dimensional or three-dimensional form?

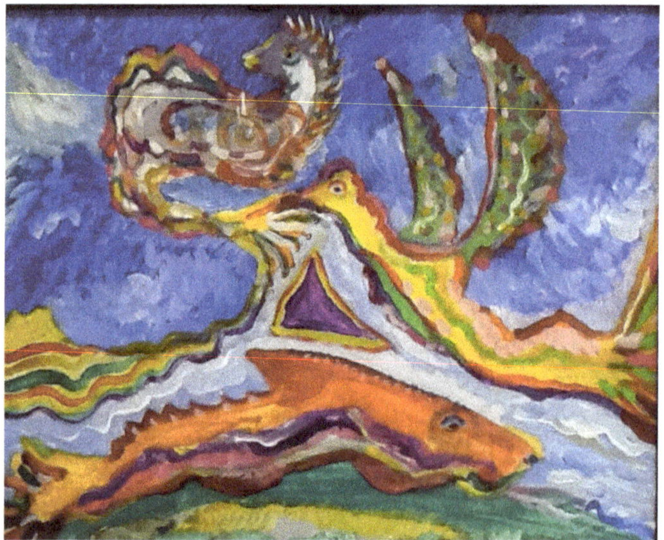

Triangle, Lynn Miller

Exploring Materials

Clay

Clay is a wonderful material. It is so earthy and feels so sensuous. It allows three-dimensional work that gives you the experience of physical touch and connection.

Oil pastels

This medium is excellent for quick sketches. The colors are brilliant and they move like butter. You can lay the colors over one another to create new colors or scratch off color to create textures. Oil pastels are also great for bringing out details in your painting after it is dry. You can also draw with the oil pastels, then apply paint washes over them. The pastels will act as a resist. Water-based oil pastels (which sound like an oxymoron) can add another dimension. You can add water with a brush to spread the pastels like watercolor paints.

Aluminum foil and masking tape

These are great materials for making 3-D objects. Shape the animals, people or figures with aluminum foil and then cover the image with masking tape. If the figure is large create the form with newspaper. Hold the newspaper shape together with tape then foil and cover with tape. The tape can be painted with acrylics or apply tissue paper with watered down glue for brilliant colors.

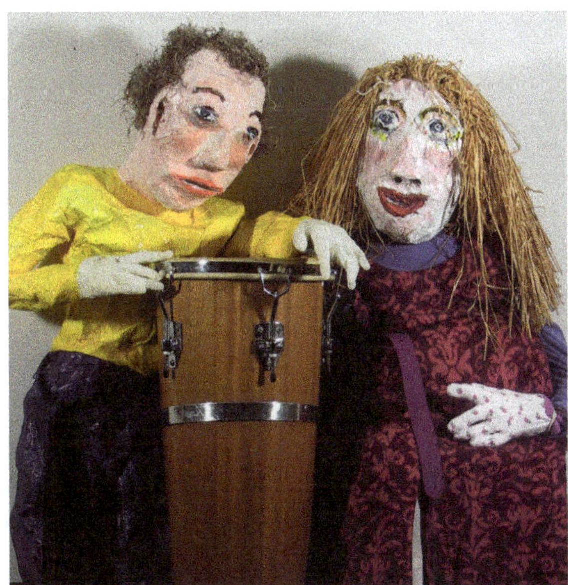

Aluminum foil and masking tape life sized dolls, Lynn Miller

Exploring clay

Shut your eyes and focus on the breath. Feel the clay in your hands then explore its textures. Play with squeezing and smoothing the clay. Open your eyes anytime and continue playing sensually. Look and feel for a form wanting to take shape. Give attention to that shape, bringing out its details.

Exploring with oil pastels

Begin by physically moving your hand over the paper. This helps to get your body involved in the process and to disengage your mind from thinking too much. Pick up the oil pastel and continue the process for Spirit painting.

Mixed media

Found objects from nature – for example, twigs, bark, rocks, feathers, grasses, and shells – are wonderful materials for intuitive art. Have wire, twine, string, yarn or glue available to bind the materials together, or use your creativity to hold them together naturally. You can add pipe cleaners, clay, paint and tissue paper to your nature materials. Don't limit your palette. Begin collecting materials for your mixed media art. Working with nature's materials – even the process of collecting them – connects you to nature. Ceremonial and ritualistic items – masks, headdresses, wands, animals, and goddesses – will often appear from art created from nature's materials.

Hanging out with images

Your images have appeared as a friend. Spend time with them. Be mindful of who you share them with. Hang out with them but have discernment which ones you leave out or share with others. Find a trusted friend who will not judge to share your images with.

There are many suggestions on how to process imagery in Section III: Arts and Healing.

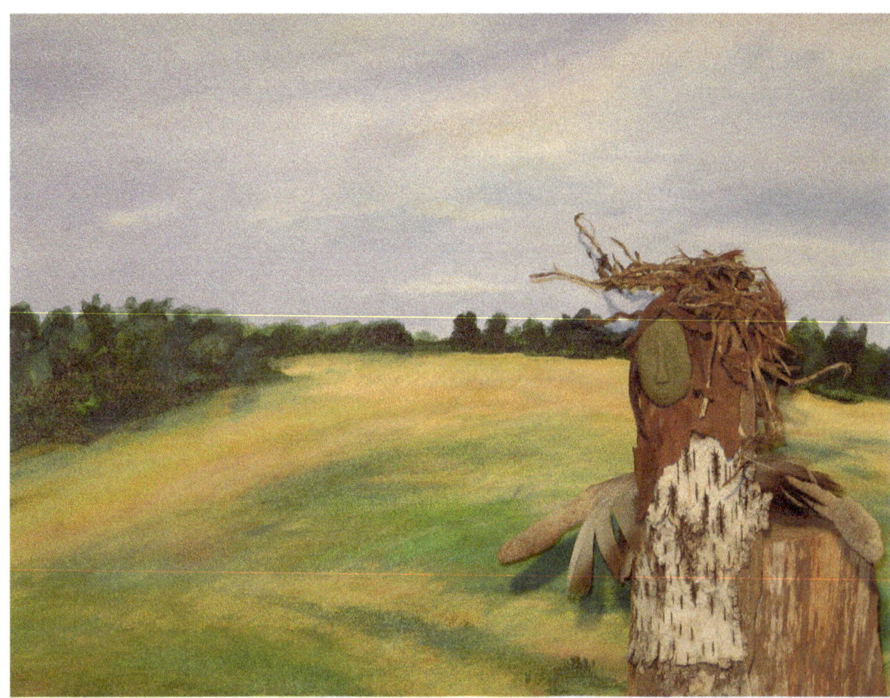

Painting and nature doll, Lynn Miller

How Music, Dance and Visual Art are Connected

Dance with your instrument, dance with your paint brush, dance with your pen

These activities are very useful as group warmups, ice-breakers and connectors. Many of the exercises can also be done by yourself for yourself.

I have always been fascinated by how different art modalities are connected. We have explored how to create authentic music, dance and art from within. Once you have experienced moving in one art form, you can translate that knowledge into another art form. Many of the elements of dance use the same elements of music and art. When creating a composition in art, music or dance - whether in a group or by yourself - it is helpful to have these tools in your pocket. The exercises demonstrate how interchangeable the arts can be once you understand the elements of a composition.

Examples will be given in **M**-movement **Mu**-music **A**-art, with some activities to articulate the theme.

Some of the same elements and concepts you will find in art, music, and dance include:

- Rhythm
- Dynamics
- Textures
- Stillness or Silence
- Imitation
- Call and response
- Ostinato

Rhythm. What is the rhythm of the composition? The rhythm sets up the feel, the style, the flavor, the feeling. Is it staccato, fluid, fast, slow, tranquil or chaotic?

M-tempo: *put drum languages in your feet, 2's to 3's to 5's; then increase the tempo.*

Mu-time signature: *play drum languages changing accents on 2's to 3's to 5's.*

A-rhythm of lines and colors: *sing drum language while drawing with an oil pastel.*

Dynamics. Are there changes in tempo, level, pitch, loudness? What is the color of the piece: is it all blue or does it have some flaring red?

M-levels: *move on the floor, move up to mid-level and end upright, with big gestures.*

Mu-loud, soft: *as a group, play as soft as you can, moving to as loud as you can.*

A-colors, contrast, light and dark: *paint transparent washes, let dry, then draw bold shapes and lines with oil pastels.*

Textures. Is it rough, scratchy, smooth, edgy, piercing?

M-feeling: *move on toes, march, tap dance, slide.*

Mu-sounds: *discover sounds by tapping, screeching, rubbing, blowing.*

A-surface: *run a comb through thick paint. Use a dry sponge or brush and blotch on color. Use a rag to pull paint off the paper. Rub pencil on paper over an object like a key to make a "rubbing" drawing.*

Find textures to imprint in clay - like leaves, netting, lace.

Stillness. Creates interest, suspense, helps you to listen.

M- *move, then freeze like a statue, begin moving again, freeze.*

Mu- *in a quartet, add your silence as a piece of the music. If everyone does same, will create duets, trios and solos – making a very interesting composition.*

A- *paint spaciously with a big brush.*

Imitation. Does it look, move, or sound like nature?

M-*follow the leader, mirror game, imitate animal movements.*

Mu-*shadow someone by playing exactly what they are playing, in unison. Imitate the sounds of a different instrument from yours; imitate bird sounds.*

A-*fold a piece of paper in half and drop colors on one side. Fold and rub - create symmetry.*

Call and Response. One person calls, the other imitates.

M-*give a movement gesture for others to imitate.*

Mu-*each person plays a short phrase; others imitate.*

A-*draw a shape, other imitates; draw and respond back and forth.*

Conversation. One calls, and the other responds with a variation.

> **M**-*move a theme, other makes a variation, continue back and forth.*
>
> **Mu**-*create a melodic line, other varies the line, continue back and forth.*
>
> **A**-*one person draws something, other draws in response; continue back and forth.*

Ostinato. Repeated pattern, repetition is grounding.

M-machine game: *each person comes in, one at a time, making a movement and sound like a machine.*

Mu-*each person comes in, one at a time, with a repeated pattern to create one sound.*

A-*each person draws, then passes their paper to the right until everyone has added to each other's picture.*

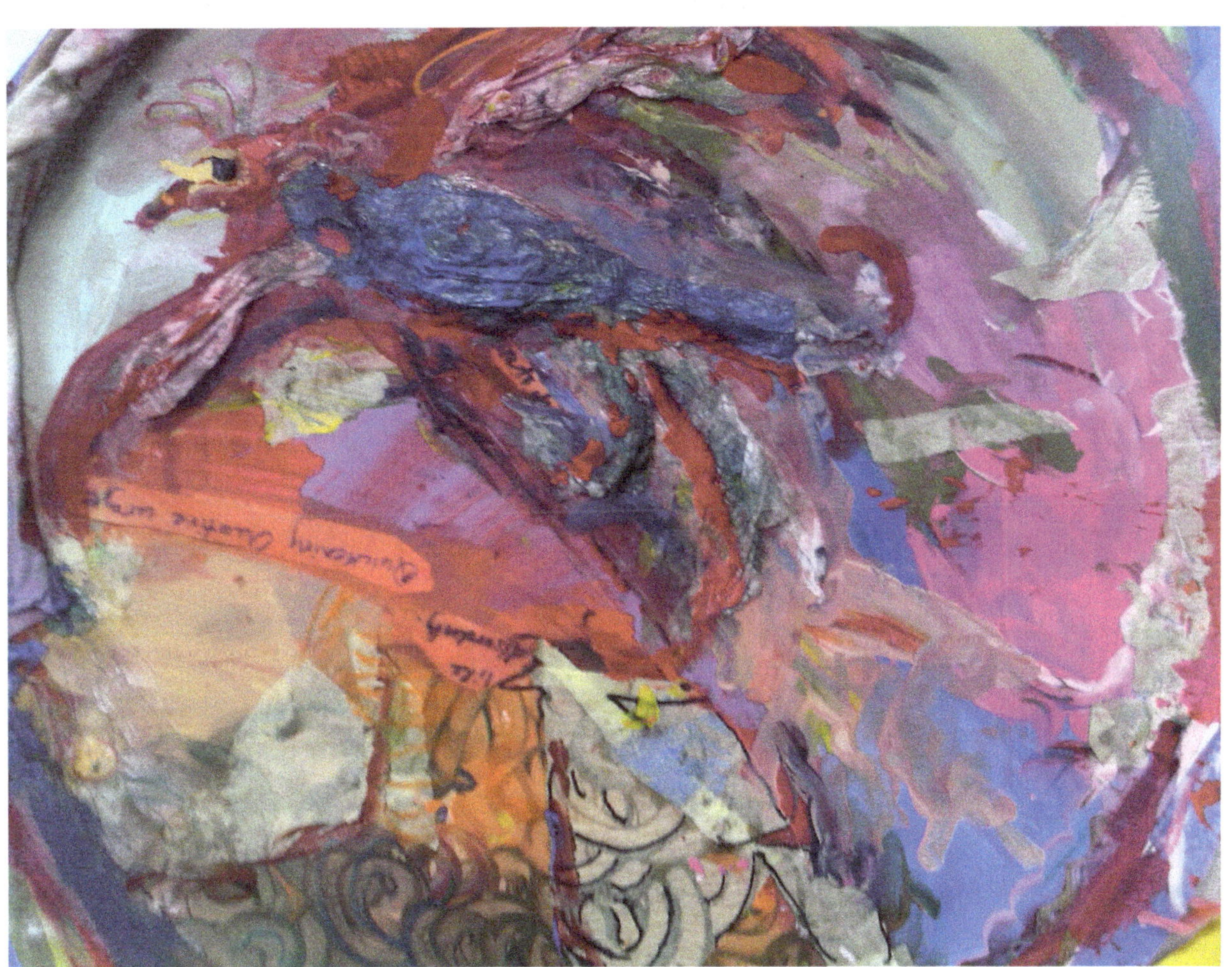

Paper Phoenix, Lynn Miller

Combining Art Forms with Groups

These group art projects help to teach the elements of the arts, cooperation and communication skills. Explorations in the Creative Arts can deepen your relationship with yourself and connection with others. These skills are adaptable for diverse ages, populations and abilities. Great way to have fun together!

Sculpting

Everyone creates figures and shapes with clay. Now sculpt a partner who remains passive as you move body parts into positions, such as arms over head, in the position of your clay sculpture. The people sculpting bring all their human sculptures together to create one sculpture. Change partners.

Negative/positive space

Dancers call off Number 1 or 2. Dancers #1 make a group shape with large spaces in between arms and legs. Group #2 fills in the negative or open spaces. Group #1 leaves their positions to now fill in the negative spaces in the shape formed by Group #2.

Make a group drawing creating large objects and shapes, filling up the whole paper. Paint in the negative space.

Create an improv dance with awareness of composition, using negative and positive space.

Group scribble

Form a circle around a large sheet of paper. Begin with movement gestures. With paint or oil pastels move the gestures to the paper with repetition. Make sounds as you make your marks. Move into one another's territories, treating all as one painting. Step back, take a look, discuss what you see.

Now tear it up. Take any pieces of it that you wish to use in your new individual collage, the beginning of your new painting.

Conducting

Everyone has an instrument - percussion, voice, or musical instrument.

Music conductor - directs instruments in and out of the piece. The conductor sets the rhythm, adds contrasts with louder and softer, brings in soloist, and makes signals for the pitch to be higher or lower. Use eye contact to be sure everyone is looking at the conductor. The conductor begins only after everyone is paying attention.

Dance conductor. The conductor is a dancer. The musicians take their cues from the movements of the dancer-conductor.

Art conductor. The musicians play what they see. The artist paints on a large paper. The musicians respond to the colors, shapes, and lines.

Free improvisation

Everyone chooses to dance, sing, or play music. Pay attention by using your peripheral vision and by listening. The intention is to create one piece. Dancers move to the music; the music is inspired by the dance; the art is inspired by the music and by the dance.

Use your imagination (this game can have many variations). One half of the group paints, while the other plays music. Paint what you hear.

Create music from what you see. Dance what you see or hear.

> We have discovered ways to use the arts - for creativity and connection to spirit, self and others. The arts are multi-dimensional, with many layers of purposefulness. They are practiced in all cultures by all ages. The arts are uniting. Now is the time to give yourself permission to be an artist, musician or dancer, if you haven't already!

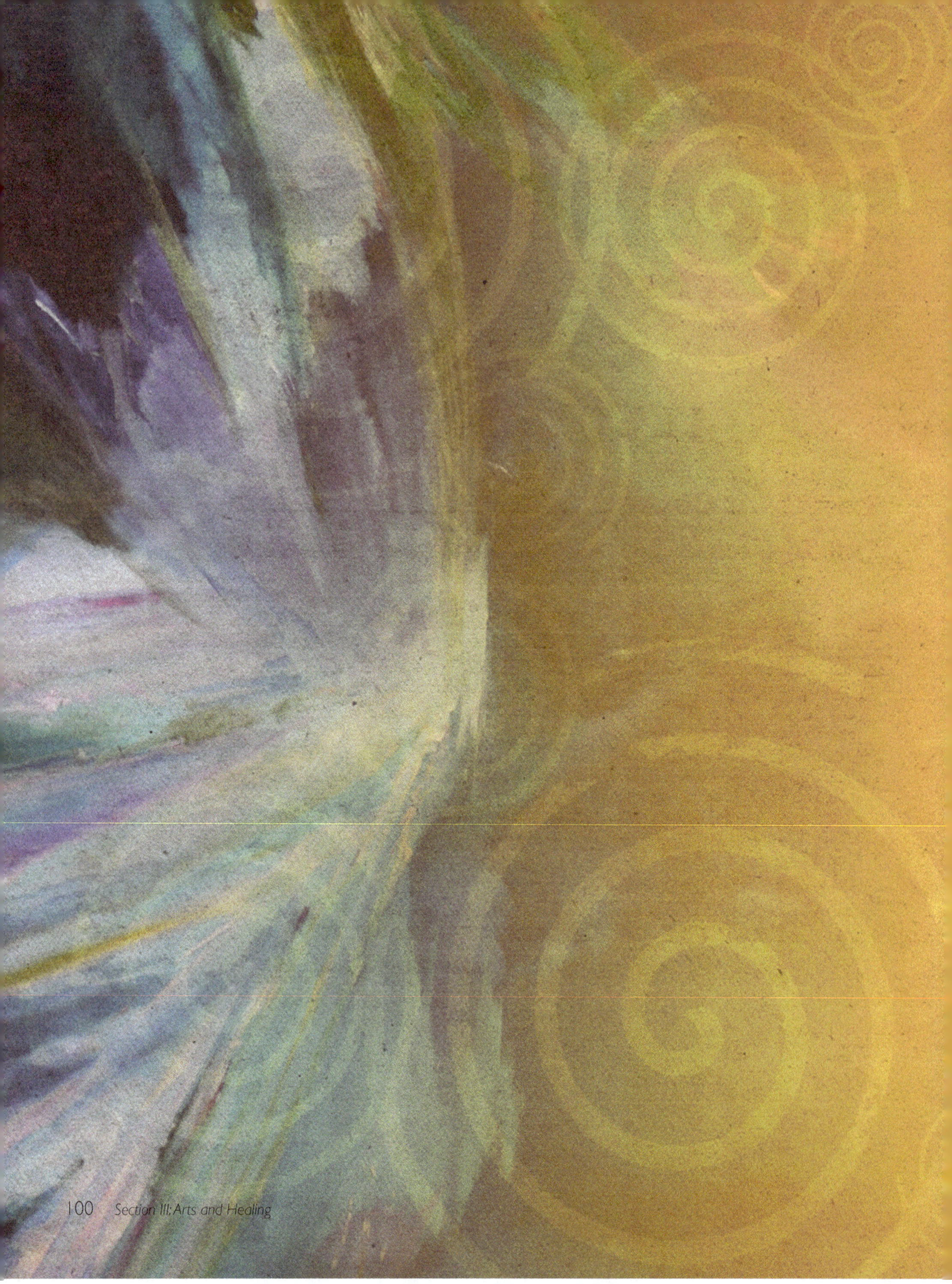

Section 3: Arts and Healing

The Arts and Healing section explores inner emotions through sound, art and movement. It is a sourcebook for therapists and for individual self-healing. Expressive therapy practices are provided for deepening the creative experience through a multimodal approach, using several art forms.

As you work with the art forms, issues may come up. Know that in order for change to occur, we must experience our emotions. Working with our emotions through the arts is a safe way to express and explore them, so we do not act them out or project them onto others. Arts are the language of the subconscious and are ways the subconscious can communicate with you. The arts can be tools to go inward and bring our deepest feelings outward and bring our subconscious ideas to consciousness. As each individual goes through the process of his/her own healing journey, there is the capacity to affect the collective consciousness. As each one of us brings awareness to ourselves, collectively we can create positive change in this world. The arts can also be used to bring to the surface ideas that are difficult to put into words. If you feel vulnerable or fragile while engaging in this process, you might consider getting some professional support.

Our culture does not always address the importance of our relationship to energy. This Arts and Healing section has a segment on energy, chakras (energy centers) and how they can be used for healing. Color and sound are used in energetic healing to bring us back to balance and wholeness. If you are a creative artist, practitioner, teacher, student or healer, it is important to learn about energy to optimize your health through body, mind and spirit. Good health is a most valuable resource. An artist and healer must be clear of interference to allow the pure spirit to come through. Learning about and working with energy helps clear any static so messages can easily come through. This knowledge can also be applied when working with others.

You will find many similarities between the methods of improvisation, healing and spirituality. The 4-part process of body-breath-heart and deep listening is the entry point; whether for arts expression, spiritual practice or healing. They are all the same path of "letting go," to be guided. The exercises: whether working through arts processes or through chakras, vibration and energy are tools to help build harmony. The arts and healing practices are to help awaken and restore that which is already there – who we truly are. All there is to do is listen.

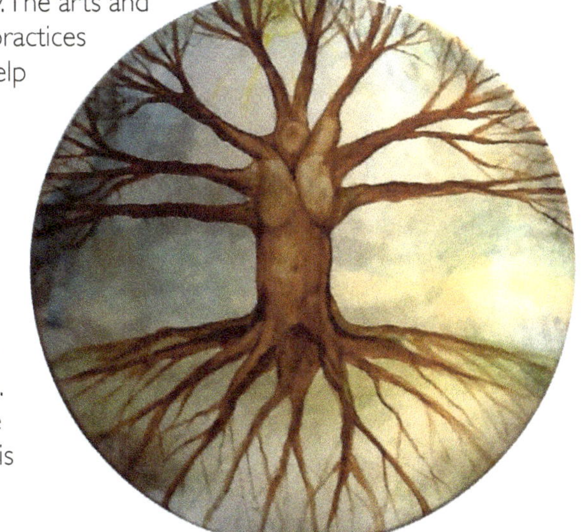

Large Healing drum, Lynn Miller

Arts and Energy as a Healing Tool

The arts have been used as a healing tool for centuries. The words art and healing were synonymous in many ancient cultures. The concept of assisting the healing process through the arts is not new. In indigenous cultures, the community worked together through ceremonies and rituals – dance, song, visual art and story telling. These community art gatherings were a container and structure for confronting fears, doubts and suffering. Music, stories, art and dance were also used in times of celebration and giving thanks.

Shamans were arts healers and messengers between the material world and the spirit world. They believed that illness was caused by soul loss. Through repetitive drumming and healing songs, Shamans went into a trance state. They went into the spirit world to retrieve lost parts of the soul. According to cultural anthropologist Angeles Arrien in ***The Four Fold Way***, many indigenous people believe that soul loss develops when we stop singing and dancing. There are many modern shamanic healers and information available on how to take your own journeys through books, such as ***Awakening to the Spirit World: The Shamanic Path of Direct Revelation*** by Sandra Ingerman.

In our ordinary reality and modern culture, soul and energy have not been taught as essential elements toward health, peace and happiness. The East has held this knowledge for centuries, contributing to ancient healing techniques using sound, movement, energy and color. Energy medicine extends back more than 4,000 years with QiGong – a Chinese practice aligning breath, movement, awareness, color healing and sacred sounds. India has also contributed to ancient healing techniques through Yoga the chakra system combining breath, movement, sound and color. These systems are used by modern healers; you can access this ancient knowledge using movement, sound and color for yourself.

When we heal, we come into wholeness, integrating the parts of us that had become separate. When we are healed we have restored integrity and balance, we are at peace. We are already whole as spirit yet we experience ourselves as living within a body. For the most part we have forgotten who we really are. The arts process is a path back to the authentic self, of re-membering our wholeness. Healing is a process, of growth experiences and evolutionary development.

Life is our palette or play in which we act out our stories in order to learn or heal. We carry our stories within us. They live in our bodies, cells, memories and subconscious. These stories are picked up energetically and read by others as a result of the decisions we make, actions we take, how we speak and how we carry ourselves. Some of our stories are hidden; some are on the surface. We may attempt to deny or repress parts of ourselves but they will speak to us through physical symptoms and mental anxieties. Energetically, we attract situations, people and experiences that help us grow and evolve. We do not always see it that way, especially if it is uncomfortable. Symptoms help reveal what needs to be examined. Mental anxieties, fears, addictions, diagnosis and breakdowns in our physical environment are opportunities for change. When we open up our inner realm through visual, auditory and kinesthetic processes through the arts, we reconnect the deepest sense of who we are. We can unbury stories that have been hidden and understand those which are revealed.

The arts speak the same language as our unconscious – nonlinear, through symbols and metaphors. Subconscious material can be communicated to us through an art form. We have perceptions in our outer world (our everyday day waking state where we interact with our environment) and our inner world (our internal feelings, dream-state, subconscious and soul). Images, symbols, metaphors and myths carry messages between the worlds. These worlds are influenced culturally, personally and archetypically. The arts express, evoke and mirror these messages. Symbolic images, sounds or movements from arts processes are translated through metaphors, myths and archetypes.

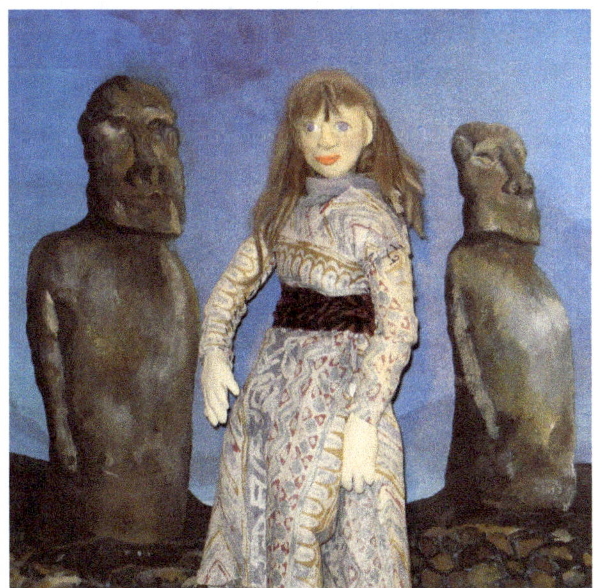

Easter Island painting and doll, Lynn Miller

Archetypes

Archetypes are collective universal imagery. In ancient times, stories or myths helped the community adjust to change. The archetypal characters (e.g., the warrior, the queen, the hero, the sage and magician) helped to build strength and moral truths. Archetypal figures appear in fairy tales and bedtime stories. The myths in childhood carried the witch, the fairy, the godmother portraying positive and negative figures. These universal figures are templates or blueprints that are here to help us grow. Each archetype can represent dualistic aspects of self. They are vessels which contain our beliefs, feelings and particular personality characteristics. They may emerge during different stages and development in our lives, such as the daughter, mother, crone. We may draw upon them without really being aware of it. They are our allies, here to show us when we are out of balance. For example, the king is powerful and has powerful people around him that he utilizes to make a strong kingdom. If the king becomes out of balance with his power, he can cause turmoil and destruction in the kingdom. When we have unresolved wounds, the activation of certain archetypes or aspects of self will become blocked. One may start as a princess, wanting to be taken care of instead of growing into the queen where she rules her kingdom. If the energy is blocked, she will always be a princess – looking outside herself for someone to take care of her. Once we realize such a pattern, the archetypes can be called upon as a helper or guide. In every stage of our growth, we have help with guiding principles through the archetypes. The more creative and loving we are, the more we are open to all archetypes. When we experience, realize or acknowledge that we carry archetypes in us (e.g., the lover, warrior, coward, child, mother and father), we realize our connection and wholeness. It is when we deny various parts that we feel fragmented or disconnected. Archetypes also come on their own behalf as a universal rather than personal energy.

The Shadow

Each archetype has a positive and shadow aspect to it. The shadow was introduced as a psychological term by psychiatrist, Dr. Carl Jung. The shadow comprises parts of ourselves that we abandoned, rejected or threw into the dark. It includes parts we don't want to acknowledge or want anyone to see. Often, we don't even want to see them so we deny them. These rejected parts usually developed during childhood. We repressed how we were really feeling in order to be loved or accepted. We may have not been given the space to have our feelings. Adults may have modeled shutting feelings down. Many adults wouldn't want a child to open up their feelings because this might trigger theirs. Many work very hard to unconsciously suppress buried emotions. True feelings are denied in order to make the hurt go away. When we throw aspects of ourselves into the dark (or hidden) through denial, we unconsciously carry the story into our life.

I grew up in a house where there was a lot of yelling. I had a fear of confrontation. I found anger a distasteful emotion and did not want anything to do with it. I suppressed it in a very nice package and shoved my own anger down so far that I did not have a clue that I had any. I would wonder what those other people were so angry about. Meanwhile, I married a very dear, yet angry, man. After he died of kidney disease and I had worked on my own healing, I discovered how very angry I was. I realized that I was attracted to an angry person to express that part of me that I could not. Of course I was also attracted to him for his many positive aspects.

The death process helped to activate my own anger. This was a precursor for me to speak up and stand up for myself. When I unconsciously want to hide my shadow self I become quiet, make myself small, have a difficult time articulating my feelings and retreat. I realize when I make myself small it is a way to hide from the shadow, angry self. Retrieving or acknowledging our hidden parts is essential for self-awareness.

Projection is when we blame others for our situations or circumstances that we cannot see in ourselves. Many are unaware that they are projecting; we distort things through the glasses of our own personal experiences. If there is something or someone we detest or repulses us, there is a good chance they are mirroring a shadow part in ourselves. We may not be so bothered by them or the situation if we have made peace with ourselves.

Have you ever noticed a pattern in your life? Could this repeated story be trying to show you something about yourself? Repeated patterns or situations give us another chance to see or work something out inside through outside circumstances. Notice who or what pushes your buttons. Who and what we attract into our lives is a reflection of ourselves, whether we see it or not.

My life story is about reclaiming my power. I "disappeared" as a survival mechanism. I was afraid of power, since my association with it was power over (e.g. abuse of power). Through arts processing, I discovered that power was not to be feared, and it is really about ***how*** power is used that matters. I had to stop shrinking to feel safe and face my fear of my shadow-to admit my own desire for power- only then could I find the healthy balance of power. I had to stop hiding and reclaim my power.

> Our deepest fear is not that we are inadequate. Our deepest fear is that we are powerful beyond measure. Williamson, 1992 (Pg. 190).

It is curious how so many people are frightened by their own power. Have you ever held your power back so others would not feel insecure around you? (this may be more of a female gesture) I love the spiritual: "This little light of mine. I'm gonna let it shine. Let is shine, let it shine, let it shine." We give others the permission to shine when we ourselves shine.

In my process, my repeated pattern has been power struggles with powerful men. I understand this is all for me to claim my power within. Yet, as I write about the shadow synchronicity has found a way for me to attract this once again as I work through the layers that spiral around this issue. My trigger relates to my father who tried to overpower me. Right when you think you have worked it out, there it is again. Sometimes our patterns may never completely disappear. Healing is when our recovery time is shorter or when we do not react anymore.

We heal when we accept a situation as part of ourselves and take responsibility for our part in the story. When we take responsibility for everything that happens to us, we take ourselves out of the victim role. We can learn and grow by changing our perspectives and make new choices for ourselves. If we are willing to look at the significance of repeated patterns in our life circumstances and take responsibility for them, we will begin to integrate the inner and the outer, our dark and our light, into one; we become integrated within. Once our shadow parts are looked at without judgment, they have less power over us. We will then respond to a situation rather than react. The dark is simply where there is no light. When we shine a light on it, it is not dark anymore. The more conscious we become on our inner level, the more we will choose to be conscious on our outer level.

Expressing Feelings

Authentic artistic expression can be a voice to express feelings, including our pain. The creative process fosters our ability to feel our feelings. Expressing what we think is negative can help us grow. It is only our judgment that makes it negative. Often we feel vulnerable when we express ourselves because we feel exposed. When we acknowledge and confront the shadow parts in ourselves through sound, movement or images, we are allowing them to be acknowledged and we are offering them opportunities for integration or transmutation. When embodying our shadow, our images, sounds or movements make their appearances to help us, no matter how grotesque or scary they may appear. Many people are fearful to open up these images, sounds or movements for fear of what they might find. The sounds, images or movements are not foes but friends. Don't censor the images, sounds or movements that want to come up in authentic expression. They are here to bring insight into who we truly are. Let go of trying to make a pretty picture, a beautiful sound, a beautiful dance. Archetypal figures may come up in our imagery to guide us, even if we think they are scary or ugly. Try an interesting experiment- ask yourself to deliberately make an ugly sound, draw an ugly picture, dance an ugly dance. You may find you can't. This ugly sound, dance or picture may turn out differently from what you expected. It may actually become quite interesting. When I ask my clients to do this exercise, it often surprises them. It can actually open up new territories or directions where one would not usually go. This can take one out of their own box, expanding insight and range of expression.

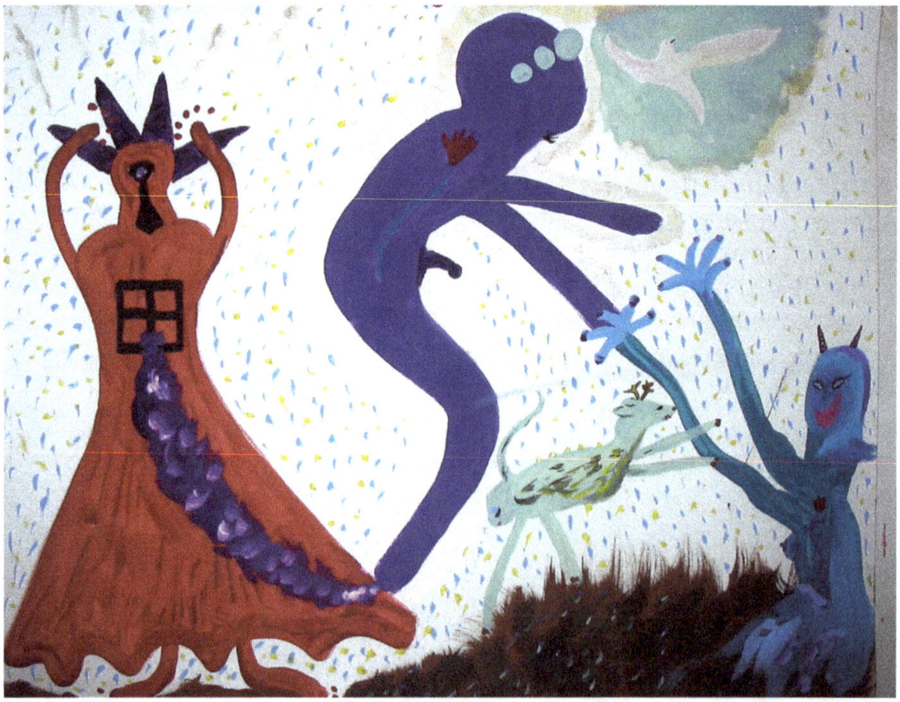

Demons, anonymous

Authentic expression is allowing what is – or allowing yourself to be. Once it is acknowledged or accepted, it doesn't need to get our attention anymore. By expressing our fragments, we are able to become whole by not denying or hiding parts of ourselves. Joy comes to us through feeling our sorrow.

When we shut down our emotions, we shut down our soul. This blocks the creative flow. Emotions are energy, carried through the soul. We are essentially electrical energy. You need both a positive and negative charge to create a current. You do not necessarily want to get rid of the negative; just acknowledge it without judgment, so it can integrate or release.

I was at a colleague's office in British Columbia – Sue Mistretta, an Expressive arts therapist. She has this sign hanging on the wall.

Express Your Feelings

Rather than try to make them go away or hide them… try

- Breathing through them
- Dancing them
- Singing them
- Painting them
- Sculpt them
- Listening to them
- Sounding (toning) them

Sounding Your Feelings

Through the voice we can release energy and emotions through sound. We naturally do this when we are hurt through groaning or moaning. In our journey of growing up, most of us were taught to be sound-appropriate (not to moan, whimper, cry, scream). This can translate into inhibiting sounds we are feeling. I had a client who suppressed her sounds during childbirth in order not to make a scene. Through both the visual art process and sounding, she was able to release the energy that was suppressed from holding in. When we hurt emotionally or physically, it is important to release sound; otherwise, this pain becomes lodged in our cells. We can clear these energy blockages through vocal sounding.

Visceral Expression

With clay in your hand, breathe in your nose and out your mouth. Connect your feet into the ground. Through the breath, connect with a feeling or emotion. Allow it to surface without censoring. Allow the energy to move through you and release into the clay. Squeeze it; squish it; make sounds. While focusing on the emotion, let a shape or form take shape. Look at the form.

Vocal Sounding

Create a sacred space for yourself. Breathe in the nose and out the mouth. Feel your feet on the ground. Take a couple of deep breaths. Breathe into your heart. Go into the feeling of an emotion. You do not need to think of a situation. Go into the feeling, not the story. Keep your breath even and move it into the feeling. Allow a sound to come out with the breath. Let the sound continue to the next breath. Continue to feel your feelings, making a sound for the symptom (feeling/emotion/lost part) in your life: What does it want to say? What does it want you to hear? What does it want you to know? Listen. Acknowledge this part. Thank it.

When we release with vocal sounding, it does not have to be loud. Even a hum can release energy that has been stuck. Take off the lid by allowing sounds, then go back to breathing in the heart area. This will create safety and will help to integrate the experience. You do not need to know what the sound is about. What is important is that the energy has moved. Moving this energy will help create change.

When our emotions are not acknowledged, we risk displacing them on someone else.

We can also release emotions through making imagery. You will need some clay for the next exercise. This can be play dough, modeling clay or potters clay.

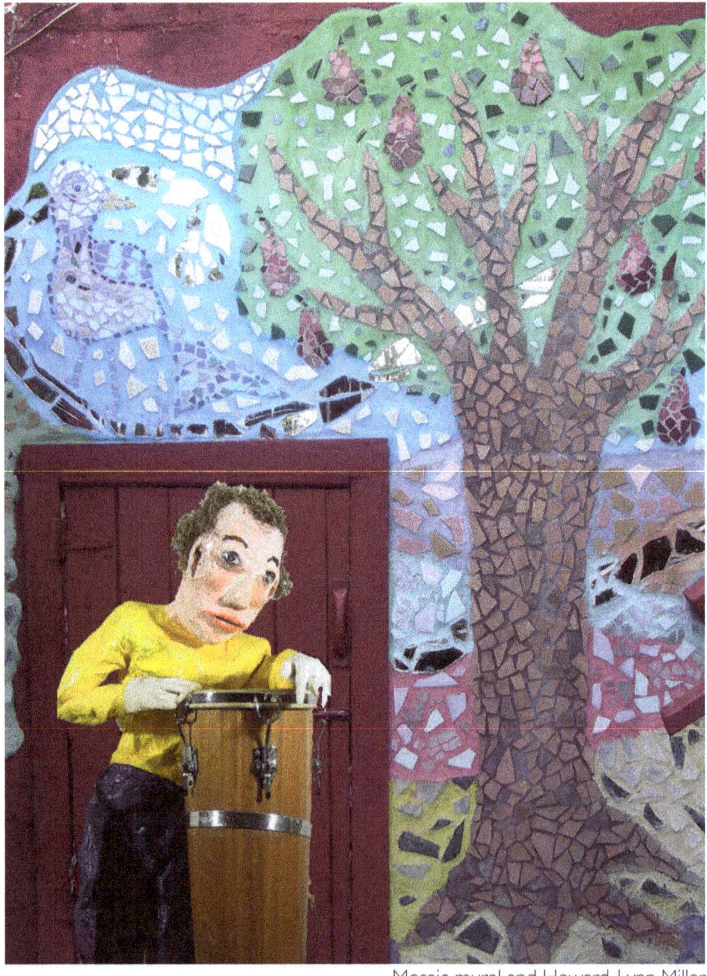

Mosaic mural and Howard, Lynn Miller

The clay gives a visceral release to help express the emotion. It is also a material from the earth which is grounding. The form that appears is 3-dimensional. You can see it, touch it. What did it feel like to release, express, or experience the emotion? What does your shape or image remind you of? Does it have a message for you?

In visual art, I look at the materials that we choose metaphorically. Clay is physical, great for anger – you can punch it, stretch it, roll it. Water colors are wonderful for grieving. Water is a carrier for helping emotions flow. Why we are attracted to certain materials is not always conscious.

I became attracted to mosaics. Metaphorically, with this art form you gather discarded plates, dishes and tiles (fragments of self) and reorganize them to create a new whole. Mosaics are much like transformation or renewal. The mosaic process begins with collecting. For months I had been collecting colored glass bottles, tiles and dishes. I knew I wanted to create a mosaic mural but could not quite find the energy. One day, I got mad enough that I dragged all those materials out of the garage and smashed them up. Guess what I was so mad about? While going to school for my masters in Expressive arts therapy, I had rationalized that I would be able to do a video project for my thesis. My advisor informed me that I would have to write an academic paper. (This is how much I resisted writing.) I'm sure there was some other repressed anger lingering around which also came out. I channeled the energy of the anger into the materials. Whoosh – between the energy, the intention and the materials, there was my mural. This was an example of transmuting the anger into something beautiful. I listened to myself – watched myself smashing the glass as I was doing it without judging, allowing myself to have the emotion. My intention to make a mural helped direct that energy up on the wall instead of a pile of broken glass in the driveway. The thesis I was required to write was practice for writing this book. Even though I resisted, it was exactly what I needed. It is important to trust the process of life, even if it is not what we thought we wanted. It is beneficial to witness self.

Self-witnessing

To witness is to deep listen, observe. To witness is to give attention or acknowledgment without fixing, advising or judging. When we have parts of ourselves that have not been acknowledged, seen or heard, they will try to claim our attention. This may be through negative self-talk – avoiding what we are really feeling, projecting, manifestation as a physical symptom or a manifestation through life circumstances. These are all signs that there is something deeper to feel or examine.

When we observe ourselves reacting, we are bringing non-judgmental awareness toward our behavior. We step out of denial when we are aware. You may find that you have more than one voice inside. These voices are often in conflict. When in conflict, acknowledge or listen to these feelings without judgment. The conflicted part will have less of a need to call for attention once the part feels seen and heard. By observing and listening within, we can validate the part that does not feel seen and heard. There is no need to do anything but listen. Once this part feels heard, it will not need to speak as loudly. Sometimes the body speaks through a symptom. Put your hand on this part, breathe into it and listen. Give it your acknowledgement and attention.

Often when we hear conflicting voices, our heart and head are not synchronized. To integrate heart and mind, go into the 4-step process: breath, connect in body, breath into heart and listen deeply. The one listening is the observer or the witness. This is the higher self, who you really are. The other voices have to do with the personality and self-identity.

Be your own witness exercise influenced by Lois Hay. Her book, ***You Can Heal Your Life*** is a wonderful guide in learning to love yourself.

This may take practice, especially if you have been in the habit of putting yourself down. Who is that? Is that really you? Who or what is underneath this criticism? Pay attention and witness this part. When we are in the witness state, we are present. Clearing comes through the breath. When you find you are not being present or are being judgmental, focus back on your breath. The breath will put you back into your body. When we breathe into the heart, we become heart-centered. The heart holds the wisdom. It can change our perspective, transmute our negative thoughts and, if we listen, bring us guidance.

Be your own witness

Look at yourself in the mirror without judgment. If judgments appear, go into your heart center and breathe through them with love. Re-program any judgments with positive statements such as, "I love and accept myself."

By being present without judging anything that arises, we will eventually feel the feelings we have locked away. Simply by allowing, we are giving acceptance. When we feel our feelings, we connect with our soul and experience compassion. It takes practice to truly listen empathetically without judgment. Make this your practice. Listen to yourself when you have gone into a place of judgment. Become the observer, your own witness. This will let the mind know you are aware. If a situation is persistent, then you know there is something deeper that needs to be accepted. Sometimes we must forgive ourselves or someone else to fully let go.

Forgiveness

Focus on the heart. Breathe into the heart. Say to yourself, "I love you. I forgive you." You may be more specific: "I forgive you for_____________".

If it is someone else who you must forgive, do the same thing. "I forgive you for not being the way I want you to be."

You cannot force forgiveness. You can continue to practice forgiveness until the energy is ready to let go. Sometimes the anger is still needed to help us strengthen to release a victim pattern to take our power back. Then it is time to surrender, to release. And let go.

Sometimes we can be harsh on ourselves such as judging and criticizing self. Begin with self when working on forgiving. "I forgive myself."

A lovely process of forgiving is through an ancient Hawaiian healing practice called Ho'oponopono. Traditionally it was practiced by a healing priest for someone with an illness. It is simple and profound. In this practice, repeat the mantra, "I love you, I forgive you, I am sorry, thank you." Say this over and over again. You may focus on what you are forgiving. Continue this practice, going through layers of forgiveness throughout your life. You may say this to the creator, your body, another or your inner child. It is even powerful to do this without any thought of a situation.

Forgiveness song

Sing a lullaby to yourself as you would sing to a child. Begin with a hum with the intention of forgiveness. Words may emerge. Sing this loving song to yourself.

Ho'oponopono Song

Sing the words I love you, I forgive you, I am sorry, thank you. Sing this as a chant, repeating the words over and over while focusing in your heart.

Nurturing Inner child

Get in a relaxed state breathe into the area of the heart and connect in your heart space. Call for your inner child to come forward by deep listening. When you can see or feel him/her, ask: How old are you? Where is the child, what is the child doing? Listen to this child. Let the child express itself. Hold the child in your heart. Hold the space for the child to have its feelings. Listen, nurture the child. What does it need? Let the child know you are here. Do not offer advice. Just be there and hold the child in your heart.

Drawing the Inner Child

Go into body, breathe into heart, call the child and listen. Connect with the child. Draw a large circle as a container. Draw a picture of the child. What do you see in the drawing? Express this drawing through movement or sound.

Inner Child

Many of us were not seen or heard as children. To be loved often came with conditions. Allowing emotions and not judging them provides the unconditional love that we were looking for as a child. The child is within us; it is in tandem with the creative spirit. This is the part of us that knows how to create. We want to make friends with this inner child. This child may also be wounded. When you find yourself reacting rather than responding, it is usually the inner child. This is the part of the child that did not get its needs met on some level. This is the part of us that needs to be nurtured and listened to without judgment. We know this part of us is feeling hurt when we are very emotional and reactive. This child will calm down once it is witnessed or seen and heard. The adult in us must help our inner child feel safe and give it the love or support it did not receive growing up. When we heal the feelings of the past, we heal the present.

The *Nurturing the Inner Child* exercise was influenced by my mentor, Elizabeth Frediani, author of ***Where Body Meets Soul.*** I grew up in a household in which I suppressed my feelings in order to survive. In my perception, it was unsafe to express yourself. You might get yelled at. When I first did this exercise, I held my child, who was a baby, day after day until she stopped crying.

Do this on a regular basis to build trust with the child, especially if this child has not been listened to. Create a relationship with this child.

Give this child reassurance if that is what it needs. Repeat a mantra, such as "You are safe;" "I love you;" "I accept you."

The inner child holds the key to the authentic self. When the child feels validated, it can reciprocate with the inner wisdom of creativity and joy. Play is a great way to have a relationship with the inner child. This is what the child wants to do.

Some were not allowed to play as children. Some were not allowed to be messy. For some, too many responsibilities were given at an early age. Many children today have full schedules with little time to play. Whatever the circumstances, you are never too old to play. If you did not get to play much as a child, you can do it now. If you loved playing as a child, you can still play.

Be an observer of yourself; be your own witness. Relax. Notice your body. Does it feel tense or relaxed? Ask: What do I need? What does my inner child need? Nurture both your child and adult into balance. This requires that you have an ongoing relationship by listening with unconditional love.

Being witnessed

There is a gift to being witnessed by others. To be heard without judgment, diagnosing, appraising, saving or evaluating can give someone the courage to explore one's authentic self. When we truly listen to someone else, we help empower them. When one is watched and listened to empathetically, without judgment, a person feels acknowledged and validated. This acceptance empowers one toward one's own solutions.

The following is an excerpt on the importance of being witnessed by Teresa Benzwie, author of ***A Moving Experience***.

> "Witnessing helps to create sacred space. Your body is truly held and supported while being witnessed which nourishes your inner world. Witnessing is a sacred art; it validates who we are, our soul, our essence. Does a tree make a sound if it is not heard in the forest? Are we truly alive if no one sees us or hears us? The witness creates the environment where we are heard in a very deep sacred way. Some psychologists say that crying by yourself does not heal the same way as crying with somebody. It validates your experience when someone hears your tears from the depths of your soul. Once we enter the sacred space, we can take it with us wherever we are and learn how to recreate it."

As we create "in the moment," we are being moved, being sung or the images come through us. This taps into both our inner world and something larger than ourselves.

Authentic Movement

Begin with the breath, close your eyes. Breathe in through the nose and out the mouth. If standing, feel your feet on the ground. If lying or sitting, feel your body on the ground. Wait for your body to move you. Wait for the impulse. Breathe in and out, allowing your body (not your mind with a preconceived idea) to move you. If the mind is interfering, focus on the breath. When you are complete, look at your witness and breathe.

Play with Inner Child

Put on some music. Get a big piece of paper, some finger paints or acrylics. Put your fingers in your favorite colors and swish them around. You could even try your feet! Make patterns and images with your hands or feet. Make it a visceral experience. How did that feel?

When we are witnessed through this process, both the witness and the creator feel a connection with one another, as well as tap into a greater universal story or collective consciousness. An important aspect of being human is the need to be connected or a part of something. We can reclaim and empower ourselves by sharing our stories with others in a supportive environment. Through being witnessed, we are acknowledged, given permission to be who we are and validated. This broadens our range of connection, self-expression, motion and emotion.

Authentic Movement

Authentic movement is a therapeutic dance form that utilizes witnessing as a healing force. Janet Adler, a founder of Authentic Movement, describes, "One of the very first experiences in life is that of being seen. The parent witnesses the infant" (as cited in Pallaro, 1999, p. 154). With Adler's experience in movement work, she noticed that being seen inevitably precedes seeing oneself. Being seen by someone helps to clarify and see oneself anew.

Authentic Movement (developed by Whitehouse, Adler and Chodorow) is a dance form composed of a witness and a mover. The mover closes the eyes, connecting with the breath to contact their inner world. S/he waits to be moved by an impulse. The mover can add sounds to gain further insights. A witness watches the mover to provide safety (not to bump into something) and holds a container for the mover to be seen, heard and felt. "The quiet focused attention of the witness helps to create a secure containing environment in which the person moving can experience a sense of being held and seen" (McGinty, 1998 p. 240). The mover is freed, for s/he is not alone on this journey inward. When we feel safe, we are freed, letting the mind step aside; this allows unconscious material to arise.

Find someone to witness your dance. This would preferably be an expressive arts therapist, dance therapist or someone who you trust.

The mover and witness come together to exchange. Movers talk about their experience, what they felt and what metaphors came to them. They may ask for comments from the witness. The witness may say, "I see you." This statement alone is very affirming for the mover who now feels seen and heard. The witness speaks only of what they saw, heard or felt, such as, "I felt like a bird flying when I saw you;" or "I felt my own sadness when I saw you." The insights from the witnesses may also bring insights to the mover.

Variations on the exchange between the mover and witness may include:

- The witness and mover draw or write what they felt after the movement.
- The witness responds to the movement with a drawing, sound or movement gesture for a non-verbal exchange.

The mover and witness then change roles. Authentic movement can also be done in a group process. One person stands in the middle and is witnessed by the group in the outer circle. The mover looks at the witnesses in their eyes after their movement. This allows them to feel acknowledged without judgment. Another group process is for multiple movers to stand in the center with their partner witness in the outer circle. The witness is to completely focus on the mover, watching for the mover's safety while watching the movement.

Being witnessed by another is a powerful experience. You may be surprised on what insights come through movements and metaphors when you are feeling held through the witness process.

The principles of authentic movement can also be applied to singing and visual art making.

Authentic Singing

When we gave voice with our first cry, we made a statement, "I am here." Authentic singing is similar to authentic movement. The singer is witnessed by a group or another person. The witness holds a container of safety and the space to just listen. When we are witnessed by another, we are held, heard and seen. Many did not always receive this in their life experience; therefore, the sounder may initially experience a release of suppressed emotions. These authentic sounds will clear an opening toward empowerment through the voice as the singer reclaims ones true self. The participant may hear ones own voice differently or for the first time.

Authentic Singing

Begin with the breath, either open or close your eyes. Breathe in through the nose and out the mouth. Feel your feet on the ground. Connect in heart, wait for an impulse. Allow sound to release without a preconceived idea. If the mind interferes, feel your feet, bend the knees and focus on the breath. When you are complete, look at your witness and breathe.

Authentic visual art making

Go to the material to which you are attracted. Use the 4-part process to center. Use your senses, feel the materials (for example, rub your hand across the paper). Focus on the sound and movement as you rub the paper. Choose a color and move it across the paper like a dance. Observe the shapes, colors or textures as they appear. Go back to your breath if you find your mind interfering. Allow the image to find its way into creation.

The witness listens intently. The person singing feels empowered by being heard and accepted. In the exchange, the witness responds with, "I heard you." The person singing shares the experience as the witness listens. The singer may ask for a response from the witness or feel complete without a verbal response. The witness responds with his/her own feelings, not what s/he thinks the person singing may be feeling such as, "When I heard you I felt….."

The singer and witness change roles after the exchange process. The witness becomes the singer, which completes the process.

Variations on the exchange between the person singing and the witness may include:

- The singer and witness move what they heard.
- The witness and/or singer draw what they heard.
- The singer and witness write what they heard poetically.
- Instruments are utilized instead of the voice.

Authentic singing can be done in a group with everyone witnessing one singer in the middle or in duos with all singers singing simultaneously being witnessed by the partner. It is recommended that the space be held by an expressive therapist, music therapist or trained facilitator.

Authentic Art

It is beneficial to work with a group or another person to witness images that appear through the art making process. Have discernment. Share your images with someone you trust. Images can be witnessed just as in the forms of authentic movement and singing.

Create images in any art form using clay, paint, found objects or oil pastels.

If the art making was done in a group, the entire group acts as the witness for each individual with their image, or the group breaks up in dyads with an art maker and a witness. Otherwise, work with a friend, expressive arts therapist, art therapist or facilitator.

Witness Dyads

Both the artist and witness look at the image intently, looking and feeling what they see.

The artist speaks first. The artist describes what the image looks like, feels like or reminds them of when they look at it. They put an "I" before each statement, such as, "I feel swirling and chaotic" or I feel red and fiery." The metaphors bring insights from the inner world or subconscious. The artist continues this process until complete. Artists may ask for a response from the witness or prefer silence. Once the process is complete, the roles change.

The exchange between the witness and artist can also be expressed through another art form such as:

- The artist or witness moves in response to the painting.
- The artist or witness sings in response to the painting.

Bringing in other art forms can change a perspective or give a new dimension to the gift of the image.

Processing Imagery Through Combining Art Forms

There are many ways to communicate with your images through combining art forms. By using all of our senses through sound, movement and visuals, we have a broader understanding of self through auditory, visual and kinesthetic input.

Once your image has appeared, look at the imagery. There is a time and place for the mind. Now is the time to bring it in to guide you. Is it balanced? Does it need more detail? Does it remind you of anything? Is it complete? As you look at your image, how does it make you feel? Your unique creation from within has come to you with a story to tell. When you ask children what they have made, they will gladly tell you a story about it, using full body expression, including sound effects. They talk about the things in the images as if they were human and able to respond back. Many of us had this innate ability. You can reclaim it or try it now if you never had this opportunity. You may be surprised by how the words flow. There is energy in the imagery that we create. The images appear as a messenger. You can communicate with, and as, your image.

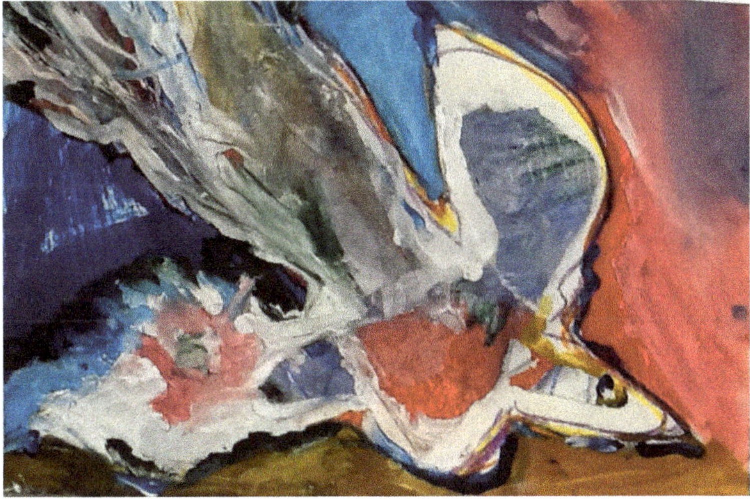

Phoenix collage, Lynn Miller

Create an image without a preconceived idea

Bring your body into the painting experience. Let the colors choose you. Which colors are asking for your attention? Begin with those colors. Physically use your whole arm, your whole body. Apply the colors mindlessly. Let the colors create the painting. The painting, not the mind, will tell you what it needs. Voice any sounds that connect you to your feelings, your body and the painting. Look at the colors and shapes; they create form.

Dialoguing

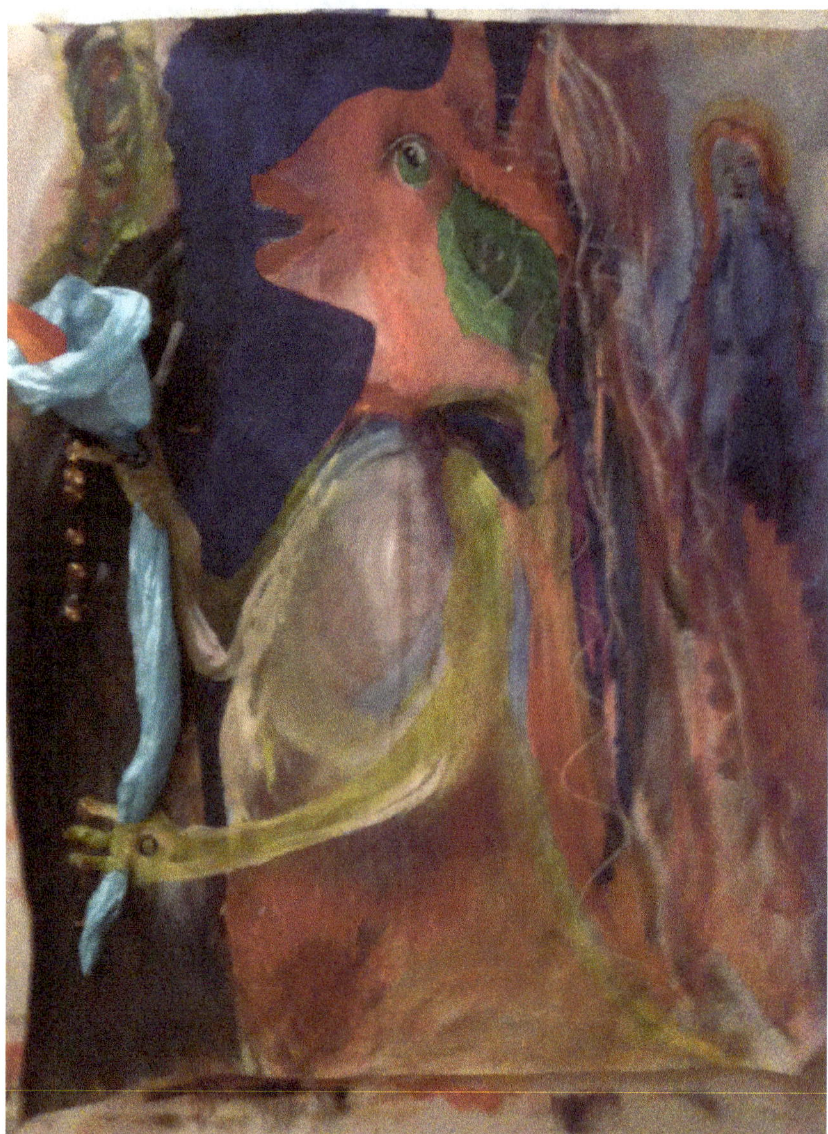
The Princess Dragon, Lynn Miller

According to Shaun McNiff, author of ***Arts as Medicine,*** images come to help us, like angels. Honor your images as sacred expressions from your soul. Treat your images as if they have lives of their own, with messages for you. Why did certain figures, animals, or objects appear in your art?

One way to find out is to ask them, ***Who are you, why are you here?*** The process of personifying and conversing with an image is called dialoguing. Become the voice for the images; let the images express themselves through you. Speak as if you are the color, shape, figure, or object in your creation. Other people can serve as your helpers – like a witness – by expressing what they see. The artist, witness, or facilitator may ask the painting questions like, "***What are you feeling? What do you need? Tell me about yourself."*** The witness may make statements from their own experience, like: "***It seems you are squished in the corner, is that true for you?"*** Be open to the mystery of what the image has to say. Look and listen from the perspective of curiosity.

> "It is all right not to know at all in a cognitive way what an image means. You will make surprising discoveries – some delightful, some disturbing. To come to an absolute conclusion about an image is to rob it of its power to guide." (***Allen*** 1995, p. 59)

Even if this experience may not make rational sense to you, allow the mystery. You may understand the process more clearly later on - in your dreams or in the future.

The Princess Dragon/ my process

I was feeling extreme anger over an incident with a colleague. He had made belittling statements toward me. I decided to process it through visual art. In my arts process, I made an intention of wanting tears because they were hiding behind the anger. I chose to paint through my feelings. I put on the music selection of Samual Barbers' ***Adagio for Strings.*** (I find this piece heart wrenching). The music helped provoke the sadness and assist me going into my hurt through my heart.

In the painting, a female figure appeared with a very sick parrot on top of her head. The watery paint dripped from the parrot's eyes. My eyes started welling up. As I continued painting, the parrot was covered up and a new mythic character appeared. The eye of the parrot was the same eye for the new figure. (As we change in the process of painting, images may change).

Once I felt the painting was complete I embodied the figure in the painting. I looked at the image and stood in its same stance. (This helps to get in-tuned with the image). Upon movement exploration I discovered the figure was a Princess dragon. The figure was holding a chalice with a fire inside. The fire was made of tissue paper, which I removed from the chalice and placed in the Princess dragons' mouth. Through a dialogue with the image (asking the image questions and answering myself) I was being guided to what the painting needed or wanted. Serendipitously I noticed there was a picture of a king on a shelf nearby. The Princess dragon was angry at the King and directed the fire that was in her mouth toward him. She was a little afraid of the fire because it can be destructive. At first she wanted to destroy the King, then realized he was belittling because of his own wounds and insecurities.

There was a female figure behind the dragon. She felt her support. While embodying the Princess, I started to sing. Initially as I sang my voice sounded young. As I continued to sing, it became fuller and louder until it filled up the entire room. The Princess felt ready to become a Queen.

When I (or the image) wanted to destroy the King I got in touch with my own anger and desire for power. It was through forgiveness, by seeing the King's vulnerability, that I was able to feel compassion for myself and the King. In real life it played out for me to embrace loving myself as well as the person who triggered me. As I embraced him with compassion the energy shifted.

It is supportive to have someone hold a safe space and act as a guide during a process like I just described. I did have peer support through this experience, as my expressive arts therapist friend was present to witness and guide the process with me. The following exercises can be used to facilitate arts processing with or without a facilitator. If something becomes too difficult to process, it is advisable to seek professional help.

Writing is a powerful form to further explore images. Cognitive exploration helps to bring the unconscious into consciousness. Try these exercises to explore your imagery:

- Give the image a title
- Spontaneously write everything that comes to mind without lifting the pen
- Look at the image and continue the sentence, I want… I have… I need…
- Dialogue with the image through writing
- Write a story about your image beginning with, "Once upon a time…"
- Write several words that come to mind after looking at the image
- Create a poem from your words

In my work in a hospital psych unit, I often use writing techniques to explore feelings with the patients' imagery. Even from the simple exercise of giving the imagery a title, life stories emerge. To write the first words that come when looking at the imagery stimulates thoughts of what the imagery is here to tell. It is always interesting how life stories emerge from the imagery. I have witnessed imagery open buried stories of death and grief as well as pleasant memories from the past. Acknowledgment of both the joy and/or sorrow helps to create movement. I have witnessed very depressed people come alive as they make connections through their imagery. Some were non-verbal in social settings. The imagery gave them a voice where they actually started to speak or it was a way to come alive in expression if language skills were lost. This process is remarkable as it fosters hope, joy, clarity, memories or truth.

It is very interesting how some people are stimulated through music and others through imagery, movement or stories. At the hospital where I work, there are people I do not always expect to respond because they sit with a blank stare. I always give all participants the opportunity; when paint and paper are put in front of some, they do respond and begin to reconnect.

Moving an image through embodying the imagery helps to understand the story it has come to tell.

- Imitate a figure or shape in your image like a statue.
- Become this figure or shape and move it.
- Connect with the emotion of the image and move it.

In a ***SpiritArts*** group, all of the participants created a form with clay. Each form was passed around the group for the group to get a closer look and feel for the piece. Each individual stood by their clay image, imitating its' shape. Participants connected with the emotion of the image and began moving and creating sounds as the image would.

Sounding an image connects with emotion and tells the truth.

- Look at the image and sing it's feeling.
- Become one of the figures or shapes and make a sound for it.
- What does the image sound like? Express it on a percussion instrument.

Drama is incorporated in telling the story of the imagery.

- Create a dramatization of the image through song, dance and spoken word.
- Tell a story through repetitious sounds, words and movements.

Repeating a sound or movement helps us to stay with a feeling so it can be fully felt and embraced before letting it go. We can connect with our inner stories through the arts, unbury those that have been hidden, and understand those that are revealed. Creating a dramatization helps keep the drama in the enactment, rather than living the drama in daily life.

Enactment

An enactment is a dramatization through an art form, or combined art forms, of a particular issue or theme that the enactor is exploring for self-realization. The theme may come out of a previous exploration of an art form (e.g., painting, movement, writing or sounding). This story sharing is witnessed by another or a community that empowers the enactor by being seen and heard. Another word for the enactment could be healing ritual. There is a deep connection with others when we make music together, paint together and move together. The arts are a vehicle for the soul to be expressed. This non-verbal communication creates a bond through each others' souls. Through a multi-modal arts approach to story sharing, we can begin to understand universal connection by exploring the process of the enactment and the witness.

Enactment Ritual

In Western culture, rituals exist around religious holidays, weddings and funerals. Historically, indigenous peoples created ritual for passages in their lives (e.g., becoming an adult or when facing hardships or celebrating joys). Many of these rituals were also connected to nature. If someone was ill, the Shaman sang or lead the community in healing songs. These rite of passage ceremonies offered community support for change. The enactment ritual is modeled from indigenous cultures that used community music, dance, and storytelling ceremonies for healing.

In the West, since there are few rituals in our culture, we must create our own ceremonies. An enactment is creating a ritual by dramatizing or telling a life story through art or a combination of art forms for healing. This is done through group support and witnessing. The purpose of the enactment ritual is to let go of denial by acknowledging and accepting all parts of ourselves. Acceptance will allow us to be an open channel for deep listening. This will bring new insight toward who we really are, a Divine being.

The following is an example of an enactment:

Esther drew a large turtle. While the group witnessed, she became or enacted the turtle by getting on the ground and making the shape of the turtle. She kept her head in the shell, putting her arms over her head and did not move. Eventually she poked her head out and moved her head around from side to side. She shared her experience with the group that through becoming the turtle, she realized she had been hiding in her shell in many aspects of her life. In her next painting she created a sea turtle that was protected by the shell but could look out and flow with the waves.

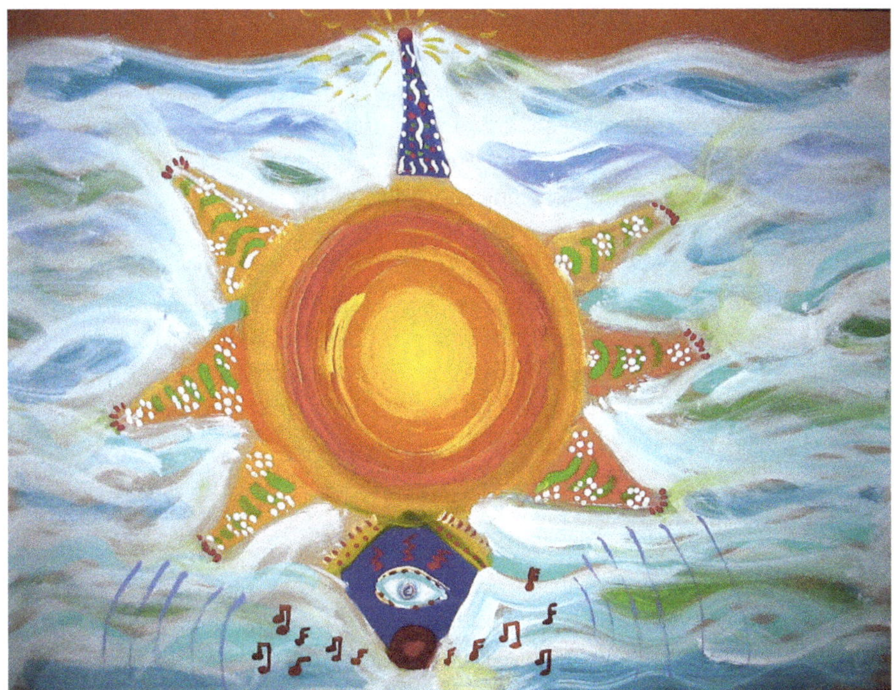

Sea Turtle, anonymous

The enactment can also include the group members. For example, have someone play drums while you move your image or have someone else move a figure from your image with you. When someone is enacting for the first time, they feel less vulnerable when others support their journey.

In a ***SpiritArts*** seminar, Sandra created a female figure with arms reaching up out of clay. She embodied the clay figure through movement and sound. She connected with the emotion of the figure through shape and sound. Her voice was lyrical and her movements flowed in and out, similar to a tide. The group formed a circle around her, recreating her sounds and movements. The participants moved toward the center where Sandra was moving and away from the center. One of the witnesses was so touched by the experience that she began crying. This shows how our stories are interrelated, how we are connected and how touched we are by feeling someone else's story and how it touches our own story.

To create an enactment ritual, the enactor sets an intention on something they want to break through, reinforce or examine closer. The enactor orchestrates the group in movement, music or dialogue to support what they want or need. There is often synchronicity in the choices when there is authenticity.

An example of an intention would be to release an emotion.

Mask-making

- *Materials: aluminum foil, masking tape, acrylic paint, feathers, yarn or other decorative materials.*
- *Cut several layers of foil in an oval shape, a little larger than a face.*
- *Create a full face shape rolling the edges or put around your face.*
- *Build up the nose, mouth, lips with foil shapes taped onto face.*
- *Cut out air holes in mouth and nose (optional).*
- *Cover the entire mask with masking tape inside and out.*
- *Paint face with acrylics, hot glue on hair (yarn, doll hair).*

Peter created a ritual for himself by lining the group up in two rows with someone playing a heartbeat drum. He built a small fire with leaves and sticks in the middle of the rows. The painting he had created earlier fell off of the easel while he was preparing the fire. He took the cue and burned his painting. During sharing, he explained that his painting represented the death of his father and burning it helped him have closure.

Beth asked the group to play joyous sounds as she leaped in the middle of the circle dancing. She cued everyone to surround her with love and caress. In her sharing, she explained that she feared pleasure. The enactment helped her to open to the possibilities of allowing pleasure into her life.

Lisa asked a participant to sit inside a box. Lisa stood behind a tree. She came out playfully approaching the person inside of the box. She danced around with colorful scarves placing them on the person in the box. She sprinkled confetti on them. She looked like a fairy sprinkling fairy dust. Her metaphor for her enactment was that she feels boxed in at work. She realized she must find a way to be creative at work or find the courage to break out of the box.

A ritual can be created to confront parts of ourselves that need to brought out. An example of a ritual to bring out an aspect of self is to create a mask that symbolizes our feminine, masculine or warrior self and wear it. Mask-making is very powerful. There is something very powerful in wearing a mask; the ego usually takes a back-seat as it feels hidden. The energy or archetype of the mask expresses itself. Masks have been commonly used in rituals in cultures such as Africa, Indonesia and Bali. Some of the scary looking masks are to ward off evil spirits, empowering the wearer of the mask.

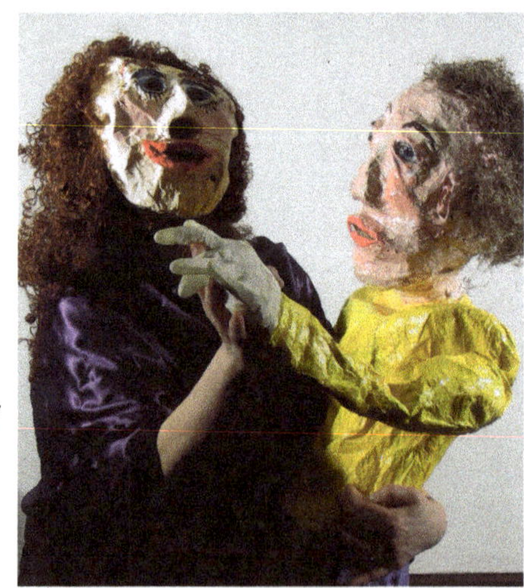

Aluminum foil mask and puppet, Lynn Miller

Another alternative is to buy a plastic mask for the form. Tape on foil to accentuate features. Cover the entire mask with masking tape, paint and decorate.

Have someone witness you put on your mask. It is intriguing for the witness to watch the mask come alive. The witness or group of witnesses can assist the process by drumming or creating sounds for the wearer of the mask. Rituals through masks can be empowering for both the one wearing the mask and the observer. Share with one another your experience of being in the mask and witnessing the mask.

With the support of the community, we remember our connections with one another through our life stories. When we step out of denial by having the courage to feel our emotions rather than stuff them, we reconnect with the spirit within. The generations before us used denial as a coping skill. This method of stuffing creates disconnect. It is essential to move out of the separation (ego based perception) and realize that we are all connected (heart-based perception). The old paradigm had its purpose – now it is time to change. The arts can support us in this change.

> When we confront or acknowledge the beliefs that do not serve us anymore we open the door to change. Art's greatest power lies in its ability to create, change and sustain life. (McNiff, 1981)

Many examples were given on ways to express feelings and emotions through the arts. Whether individually or in a group process, it is you that must do the work. The process is not always easy but arts processing can turn that work into play as you begin to feel more joy after expressing that which had been pushed away. As we confront what does not serve us anymore, we shed our densities, opening to more light and higher vibrations.

Healing Vibrationally

Everything in life is energy or vibration. Vibration exists in all things. We may look solid but we are made of vibrations. We are all connected through energy or vibration. Sound is vibration, color is vibration and we are made from vibrations. Animals, trees, rocks, chair, house – all have a vibration. Even our thoughts are vibrations. Have you come across someone with whom you feel a resonance or another a disharmony? There is an energy charge with the vibration of every thought. Therefore, it is important that we be conscious of our thoughts. What we think about or give energy toward will be attracted to us. This can be in the form of people, places and situations. Vibrations with like frequencies resonate or attract one another. By raising our thought vibrations, we can attract what we want in our lives. It is most important to be aware of what is being sent out through thoughts, for what comes back is a vibrational match.

Every vibration has a frequency. Frequencies are the rate of vibrations. There is a frequency in our cells, organs, thoughts. When we are out of balance, we come out of tune. When we are out of balance, we feel a disharmony. This disharmony can manifest as pain, stress, tiredness and confusion. This is our body speaking to us, a signal for us to look at something, feel something, notice something. Imagine the body as an orchestra. Is something out of tune? This lack of harmony may be expressed as a symptom. Sound and color work vibrationally and can retune us back to wholeness. As we clear out our negative thoughts and beliefs through emotional release (discussed in the previous chapter), we make room for frequencies of love and joy. When we focus on harmony – what is right rather than what is wrong – we create a resonance that connects with spirit or life energy. When we are in harmony with spirit and nature, we are in tune.

Entrainment and Resonance

Entrainment and resonance are basic principles of sound healing. In 1665, a Dutch scientist, Christian Huygens, found that when he swung two clocks next to one another, the pendulums would eventually synchronize. Entrainment occurs when a weaker rhythm synchronizes with a stronger rhythm. You may have experienced a drum circle in which people are playing at once without deep listening. Chaos could occur but, eventually, the drums will entrain into an order. Some claim that our brainwaves entrain to the electrical system where we are living. In the US, we entrain to the frequency of 60hertz, 60 cycles per second; in Europe, the body entrains to 50 hertz, 50 cycles per second.

Sound is vibration and our body systems entrain

to music. Entrainment occurs when two vibrations come into resonance. Resonance is when a vibration sets off a similar vibration in another body or object. Resonance occurs when energy is transferred from one frequency to another; this causes it to vibrate. An example is when a violin plays a C near an opened piano, the C string will vibrate the C string on the piano. Through entrainment and resonance, sound can be used to harmonize the body. The frequencies in the body or mind entrain with the frequencies of sound. Music can tune up an out-of-tune frequency in the body. When a sound is introduced, the body will attempt to entrain or vibrate at the same rate of the sound. Music can also entrain our emotions. Have you ever felt stressed out and put on relaxation music? You might notice deeper breathing and relaxation. Research has shown that sound can lower blood pressure, increase respiratory rate and calm the nervous system. Our brain waves also entrain to sound creating different states of consciousness. Beta (14-20hz) is our alert working brainwave; Alpha (8-13) is relaxed; Theta (4-7hz) is meditative; and Delta (1-4hz) is the sleeping state. My husband, Dr. Eric Miller has written a book, ***Bio-Guided Music Therapy.*** This is a practitioners guide to the clinical integration of music and biofeedback. Through biofeedback heart rate, muscle tension and blood volume can be measured. Brainwave activity is measured through EEG. Through the combination of music and biofeedback, his practitioners develop skills in managing or improving their physiological functions.

In the hospital where I work as a music therapist, I use music to assist people with pain management and anxiety. When someone needs to be lifted emotionally or spiritually, I play rhythmically faster music; when they need to relax, I play slower melodies. Depending on what is needed – to stimulate or to calm – different instruments are used. The voice and native flute are used to calm. The music helps to relax not only the patient, but the doctors, nurses, transporters, maintenance and cleaning people. The patients and staff usually say that the music helps them feel less stressed.

When I am working bedside with someone in pain, I pay close attention to their breathing. I often match the rhythm of the tones to the rhythm of their breathing. To induce relaxation, I gradually play slower and fewer notes. Usually the breath entrains with slower fuller breathing; often, the person falls asleep.

If someone needs to be lifted emotionally or spiritually, I play the guitar and invite the patient to sing or play a shaker. Because music is individual, I ask their preference of style. I have witnessed people who were at the hospital for failure to thrive come alive as their soul engages with the music. In our culture, many people do not have the opportunity to sing unless they are in a choir, such as in church. Many elderly are unable to attend church and lost this gift. When they engage in singing, their affect changes and brightens. The music I assist people with in the hospital has helped people receive fewer medications for pain and anxiety.

Before becoming a music therapist, I first explored sound work when I worked in a group home for developmentally delayed adults. Two of the clients were nonverbal. I often imitated them in an attempt to communicate. When I matched what they did, there was usually a response. Many of their movements and sounds were humming and rocking, which was termed self-stimulating. When I tried this, I found it very relaxing. Many years later, I took a training at Don Campbell's Therapeutic Sound School. Don was a pioneer in sound healing and author of ***Music: Physician for Times to Come***. In our sound explorations, I made some similar discoveries I had made when imitating the people in the group home with a method that is termed toning.

Toning

Our voice is the most healing instrument of all. Unlike other instruments, it has consciousness and is the instrument of the body. We can create self-generated healing and assist others by moving energy through toning, or vocal sounding. The vibration of the tone creates an internal massage. This movement of energy can ease physical pain and relax the body. Through toning, mental, physical and emotional blocks can open through sound vibrations. Toning can ease the mind, opening spiritual connection. I often use toning as a form of meditation and centering. I find it difficult to run an inner dialogue and tone at the same time. Toning helps to quiet the mind. This quiet opens one up to deep listening. After toning for fifteen minutes, it is always fascinating to sit in silence afterwards. As I listen, I hear things more acutely, with more awareness than before the session. The listening opens us to the inner, intuitive voice. Toning helps to learn how to deep listen – one of the steps in the four-part process.

One approach to toning is through long tones of vowel sounds. At the Therapeutic Sound School, our coursework included toning the vowel sounds ay, eee, ah, oh, ooo. We toned them lying, sitting and moving, exploring one vowel per day. You may try this to deepen your exploration.

When toning, go inside the sound. Feel the sound; listen with your body.

When making tones, notice where they vibrate in your body. Listen deeply to the sound. Does the tone change? The vowel sounds set up resonance. As mentioned in an earlier chapter, the vowels carry spirit.

Explore making long tones, any sounds that want to be expressed. Does the sound get raspy or clearer with different sounds? Are some tones more difficult to get the air through and others with more ease? Notice the location in the body where the sounds have less ease. Put your hands on this place. Toning can be used to release pain and emotions. Send the sounds with intention to this area of the body or intuitively make sounds from this area of the body.

Toning Using Vowels

Experiment with different vowel sounds – A, E, I, O, U – used with intent and see where they touch you.

Toning for pain release

- *Place your hands on a symptomatic area of the body. What does this discomfort sound like?*
- *Tone what the pain sounds like. What does this symptom want? Create the sound that would sooth the symptom. This tone can be quiet like a gentle hum. Allow for what sound is needed for balance.*

Vocal Scanning

While in the Therapeutic Sound School, we made and taped a vocal scan daily for several months. A vocal scan is a siren technique. Sing from your lowest note to the highest and come back down. What are we listening for? Were there bumps, was their much range? Did the sound jump leaving out sections? Were there emotional accents or twitches in the body?

Vocal scans move energy and sound vibrations up and down the body. Are there places where the energy is stuck? Does it help to move the eyes up and down, or to focus forward? Does it help to move the arm up and down as one sings up and down? All of these observations help to "tune in" and deep listen.

When working therapeutically with a vocal scan, I often notice that people jump a whole section in their range. They may start low, jump the mid-range and go right to the higher register or start low and stop at the mid-range. They are directed to listen for where the sound jumps and stop at this place. This helps the participant listen within. I ask them to fill in the missing tone where the sound jumped or broke. Pulse this note, until it feels clear, then slide it slightly up and down for integration. Continue to scan and repeat the process, if necessary. Vocal scanning helps to move energy and awareness into places we may have subconsciously avoided or not given much attention to within our energy system.

I also use this scanning method when guiding people to discover a deep place within when exploring the authentic voice. I have witnessed some profound openings through this method. Participants sing scans and stop where they hear a jump or where the tone changed or became gravelly. They are directed to connect with the feeling in this space, then fill in the note, pulse and allow the sound to go into a soul song from this place. People have made breakthroughs with this method in singing from their truth.

Elizabeth Laurel Keyes was a pioneer in toning with her book, ***Toning, The Creative Power of the Voice.*** Her toning group toned healing for themselves, and others. Through intention, they were able to help others with long distance healing. The vibrations were sent through with their intent. Setting an intention is an important aspect for directing energy for the healing process. Elizabeth had a toning group in which they sent sound long distance with miraculous results. Experiments have been measured by Naturopathic doctor and molecular biologist Dr. Adam McLeod through EEG that show that our brainwaves are altered by intentions of others. Physiology can change from our own thoughts and be affected by the thoughts of others. When we set an intention, we are calling the Divine to assist us in the healing process.

Masaru Emoto in ***The Power of Water*** has some profound photographs of water crystals changed by words. Words like "no good" and "unhappiness" pasted on a bottle of water, frozen and then photographed, showed pictures of crystals that were not fully formed. Words such as "well done" and "happiness" formed beautiful crystal patterns. His theory is that 70% of the human body and much of the earth is made up of water. Therefore, energy can be transmitted through water with intention. Through good intention, gratitude and love, we can transform the planet with water as our conduit.

In ***Medicine for the Earth,*** Sandra Ingerman, an educator on shamanic studies, brings to our awareness how important the words are that we say to ourselves or out loud. Our words can create the intent to heal or create illness. We move out of the Divine inside if we say things that are against our perfection. With this theory, we can change ourselves and the planet through transmutation (a process of letting go of ego and surrendering to the Divine within). It is our egocentric mind that creates limitations. To heal, we must be open to the possibilities, open to miracles.

I took a workshop with Jonathan Goldman, soundhealer pioneer and author of ***Healing Sounds***. He demonstrated a sound healing sirening technique that Elizabeth describes in her book on toning. Toning can be used with intention to resonate different areas of the body for healing. Jonathan created the formula, sound + intention = healing. The practitioner begins the session with an intention such as, "May I be guided by the Divine, may these sounds be for the highest good." The practitioner slowly sirens up and down the body of the person coming for a treatment. The practitioner either senses a thick or sticky area, hears a change in the resonance or intuits where the sound is needed. The practitioner directs sound in this area. They are guided through intuition, rather than thinking what would be a good sound or key. The practitioner pulses the sound in this area until it feels clear. This technique has helped others release pain and physical symptoms. Toning helps move energy that can clear the aura and the chakras.

Resonating Chakras with Vowel Sounds

There are several systems toning vowel sounds for resonating and balancing chakras.

The chart below is a system devised by Joy Gardner author of ***The Healing Voice, Traditional and Contemporary Toning, Chanting and Singing*** (p.126). Experiment with your own sounds along with the sounds given in the chart. Remember to begin with diaphragmatic breathing. Sing the sounds slowly in whatever pitch feels comfortable. Direct each sound to the specific area of the body. Try a low tone for the 1st, 2nd, 3rd. Can you feel any vibration? Try a higher pitch for the 4th, 5th, 6th. Experiment with directing the tones focusing on sensing energy in each of the chakras. Sing the tones slowly.

Chakra Sounds

1st Chakra	Root (Sacrum)	E (as in red)
2nd Chakra	Belly	O (as in home)
3rd Chakra	Diaphragm	AOM (amen & home & mom)
4th Chakra	Chest	AH (as in hah)
5th Chakra	Throat	UU (as in blue)
6th Chakra	Brow	MM (as in mom)
7th Chakra	Crown (Top of Head)	EE (as in glee)

Chakra Balancing through Emotional and Body Awareness

To be in the moment, deeply listen and be a clear channel for spirit; it is important to keep our energy centers, or chakras, fine-tuned. The chakras are spinning energy wheels located from the base of the spine to the top of the head. They are responsible for distributing energy going in and out of the body. They manage our life force energy for mental, emotional, physical, creative and spiritual functions. Due to life circumstances, the chakras become blocked. During different stages of our development, we may not have received the support for the chakra to develop clearly. We may have shut down our energy in order to protect ourselves from trauma and childhood difficulties. Patterns and belief systems develop that may not serve us anymore, yet we continue to operate in this way of being and with a compromised chakra. When one chakra is out of balance, it can affect the others.

Emotional awareness

The chakras are seven consciousness centers. When our chakras are balanced we are (1st) grounded (2nd) have personal boundaries (3rd) advocate for self (4th) willing to give and receive (5th) speak our truth (6th) listen to higher self and are (7th) guided by the Divine. When a chakra is out of balance one is emotionally compromised. Life is a school full of lessons. Our life circumstances begin the pathway for our learning journey. The chart below describes the consciousness of each chakra and the symptoms when they are not in balance. Our emotional make up helps direct us to which chakra needs attention.

	Balanced Chakra	**Unbalanced Chakra**
1st	grounded, safe, in body, prosperous	ungrounded, victim, out of body
2nd	creative, connected to others	controlling, sexual trauma
3rd	self advocate, self assured	low self esteem, shame, egotistical
4th	feel feelings, compassionate	shut down, angry, resentful
5th	speaks the truth, creative	unable to confront or express self
6th	clarity, connected to inner wisdom	overly analytical, confused
7th	spiritual connection, guided	disconnected, does not trust

Witness your emotional patterns. Which chakra needs more nourishment? Completion of emotional issues help to clear the chakra. Many of the emotional clearing ***SpiritArts*** exercises help to obtain this completion through arts processing. Balancing the chakras is a life process. Awareness is a key.

Our thoughts are energy. Giving love and support to yourself will strengthen the chakra. Positive statements help support compromised chakras. Here are some statements to try. Create your own. Remember the words we say have power.

1st chakra: "I am strong, I am safe, I am prosperous."

2nd chakra: "I am creative, I am me. It feels good to be me."

3rd chakra: "I am powerful, I am confident."

4th chakra: "I love myself, I am compassionate."

5th chakra: "I am willing to speak the truth. It feels good to express myself."

6th chakra: "I trust my intuition, I am clear."

7th chakra: "I am guided by spirit, I am connected, I am one with the Divine."

Repeat them as a mantra. Sing them as a chant. Create your own personal statements. When you find the one you need, repeat it over and over, especially if you are feeling compromised. Notice if you begin responding differently through positive self-talk.

The chakras will heal as we give them awareness, give ourselves love and support and complete unresolved issues. Some may be chronic and may need attention to evolve. Pay attention to your own personal stories around each chakra. Write your personal story around each of your chakras. This will help you identify your developmental history and awareness toward what needs release or strengthening for balance and self -actualization.

This is my story identifying a chronic 5th chakra issue:

When I was a little girl, I was afraid to say anything (5th chakra). I was afraid that it would be wrong or that I would get yelled at or shamed (3rd chakra). I constantly had earaches and sore throats (5th chakra). My biggest fear throughout life was to confront others. I made myself small so I would not be noticed (3rd chakra). I did not feel safe (1st chakra).

This is how I nourished my 5th chakra to help it heal:

I loved to sing. Even though I was yelled at to stop making that noise, I continued to sing because it made me feel good. I explored every part of my voice without judgment – the pretty and the so-called ugly voices. When I became stressed, I would release the energy through sounds. In the process, I stepped back into my body, widened my range, developed my singing voice, listening skills, courage and discovered who I really am. I went from a person who was afraid to say anything to a performer who could stand up in front of hundreds of people to express myself and sing my song.

When I am out of balance, many of those old feelings can return. The exercises prescribed in this book are what help to obtain balance or are tools to bring one back when they are out of balance. The body is very smart. The body knows. We just have to listen to it.

Body awareness

Our body is our messenger. Do you feel physical symptoms? Our body is speaking to us. What chakra is the symptom located near? When we experience symptoms (physical or emotional) it is simply our body speaking to us. Since our organs and endocrine system are connected to the chakras, try and locate which chakra is located nearest the symptom. Symptoms help guide us toward which chakra needs attention. Send extra energy to the chakra that is associated with the compromised organ.

	Chakra location	**Organ associated**
1st	sacrum	kidneys, adrenal glands, spine
2nd	belly, below belly button	spleen, bladder, kidneys
3rd	solar plexus, midriff	pancreas, liver, stomach
4th	heart	heart, immune system
5th	throat	thyroid, lungs, bronchial, ears
6th	3rd eye, center of forehead	vision, head, brain, pineal gland
7th	crown, slightly above top of head	pituitary gland, nervous system

Begin by placing your hands on the location or several inches off the body for each of the chakras. Breathe in and out, noticing any sensations, tingling or movement. Start from the first and work your way up to the crown. The more you do this, the more you will connect with the energy.

You may talk to the chakra or ask if there is anything it wants. Chakras like to be seen and heard and acknowledged like the rest of us. Does it want to release? You can do this through sound and movement. Identify a chakra that would like attention, allow any sounds and movements to release from this area. Does it want to be soothed? If so, give a gentle massage and soothing sounds to the area. As you become more in tune with your chakras, you will energetically feel when they are out of balance. Give them the attention they are asking for.

QiGong, Yoga and Thai Chi are movement practices that move life force energy. They are all great practices to help nourish and balance the chakras, organs, and the mind, body, spirit connection. You can also move energy through dance. Put on some music and move!!

Chakra dance:

- *Play some rhythmic music.*
- *(1st)Feel your feet on the ground, dance with your feet, what can you do with your feet?*
- *(2nd) Rock the pelvis, dance with your hips, making a figure 8 movement.*
- *(3rd) Isolate and move only the midriff, keeping hips still.*
- *(4th) Slowly roll the spine down touching fingers to the floor. Slowly roll up, opening arms and chest while toning ahh.*
- *(5th) Move head slowly looking up, down and side to side, then figure 8.*
- *(6th)Move the eyebrows up and down.*
- *(7th) End in stillness and focus on the crown opening.*

Share gratitude to each of the body parts. "I love my belly." Even the parts we wish were different. Especially thank that part. If it is symptomatic, give an apology for not listening to it. "I am sorry I did not listen to you." "My body is strong and healthy. I love my body." Think about the function and miracle of each body part such as, "I love my feet, they help me walk through life." Our body and all its parts have consciousness. It is through being in our body that we heal and connect with the Divine within.

When we are healing on the physical level, it is important to clear the emotion, make friends with ourselves, visualize the body part healthy and feel the emotion of what it would be like to be completely healed.

If you could not feel or imagine yourself without the symptom, look at how this symptom is serving you right now. Continue working with clearing emotions associated with the body part through sounding, moving, drawing and journaling. Strengthen the connection of feeling balanced through sound and color meditations.

Physical healing Meditation

Take three deep cleaning breaths. Breathe slowly into the heart until you are in a relaxed state. Imagine what it would be like to have your symptom disappear. Who would you be without the symptom? See and feel yourself fully healed.

Balancing the Chakras with Sound and Color

Sound, color and crystals have strong vibrational energy that can strengthen and move energy in the chakras. These modalities work vibrationally, resonating at the same frequencies as the chakras. Our bodies entrain with these vibrations. Visualize the color or sound balancing the chakras. Intention helps to focus and amplify the energy. Imagine the sound and colors restoring balance and helping to clear any old energy.

There is not just one system for healing the chakras through sound and color. The resources are conflicting as to the color or pitch for each chakra. We are all individual; there is not one size fits all. Try these suggestions on for size, as a reference point. Listen to yourself for what sounds or colors your chakra needs or wants.

Sargam as Chakra sounds

My favorite system is singing the Indian sargam syllables. You have all heard and probably sung the major scale with solfege syllables – do re me fa sol la ti do. Solfege uses the do re mi symbols for sight singing. The Indian equivalent (sargam) uses the sounds Sa Re Ga Ma Pa Dah Ni Sa in Indian classical music. These ancient syllables are sacred Sanskrit sounds. Each syllable is connected to a deity and an animal. The sargam syllables have a pure resonance. I find the sargam syllables are the perfect placement of the mouth to make the purest tone for the pitch. The resonance is what assists the chakra. The vibratory patterns of the chakras are in tune with the seven notes in the major scale (C D E F G A B). We will add the octave C for completion. A lower sound has a slower number of vibrations per second and a higher sound has a faster number of vibrations. Our bodies vibrate in sympathy with these sounds. Do not be confined to singing from C to C. Your range may feel more comfort from G to G. Focus on the sound. It is the sound that will take you on a journey and into a relaxed state. This is a powerful exercise to sing against a drone such as a shruti box or other sustaining instrument tuned to a fourth or fifth.

Pitch	Solfege	Sargam	Chakra	
C	do	Sa	First	base of spine
D	re	Re	Second	pelvis
E	mi	Ga	Third	solar plexus
F	fa	Ma	Fourth	heart
G	sol	Pa	Fifth	throat
A	la	Dha	Sixth	third eye
B	ti	Ni	Seventh	crown
C	do	Sa	Octave	above crown

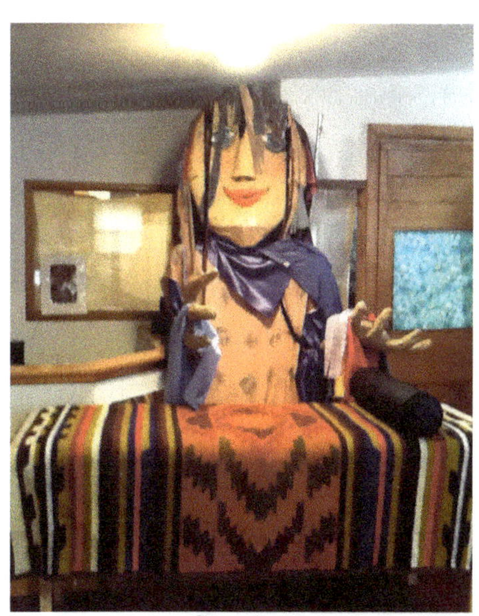

Chakra healer puppet, Lynn Miller

First sing the major scale with the do re mi syllables to get the familiarity. Now sing each note very slowly with the sargam syllables. Sing each note as a prayer. As you sing the note, connect that note with the area of the body where the chakra is located. Place your hand on or near the body in the chakra location. Deep listen as you sing the tone. Singing the scale slowly will tune your ear and your body creating a sound body connection. Once you have sung up to the octave, sing the scale descending Sa Ni Dah Pa Ma Ga Re Sa. If a chakra is feeling distressed, lay on the tone for that chakra, such as a headache, slowly repeat Dah. After completion of singing the scale slowly up and down, make a slide or sirening sound up and down the scale with the syllable Sa. This helps with integration. Notice what chakras or sounds you are most drawn to. How is your Ga today? Is your Pa strong? Are you feeling it in your Ma? Listen to your voice tone. Is it pure or a little week at certain chakras.
A 20-year-old autistic woman comes to see me for chakra balancing for impulse control. She is quite brilliant and knowledgeable about chakras on an intellectual level. On the other spectrum, she has fascinations and interests of a six-year-old and can act out frustrations as a two-year-old. She has difficulty adjusting to change, especially to her routine. She can act out tearfully or aggressively. She has perfect pitch and is quite in tune with music. We begin our session singing the chakra sounds in sargam as a tune-up. When she is singing in the session, her true essence and brilliance shines forth. Her mother says that she uses her chakra sounds and knowledge of them to help self-regulate when she is at home.

When singing the major scale slowly connecting the sound and syllable to each chakra helps to train the ear. If you move your hand up or down with the sound it gives a reference point. Is the note high or low? Visualize the sound climbing up or down a ladder or keyboard up your spine. Is one sound close or far away in relation to another? The distance between notes is called an interval. Notice how each syllable and interval feels in the body.

What is really interesting about Indian music is the microtones or notes in between the notes. This exercise is for those who want to develop their musicianship. Slowly slide between Sa and Re and back to Sa, using your hand to visualize the distance between this interval. It is close. While sliding, listen to all the in-between notes. Do this several times. Even though it is close, it can feel a distance as these sounds take you to an infinite space. Get this sound into the body – where it is, how it feels in the body. Go to the next interval slowly sliding from Sa to Ga and back to Sa, using your hand. Visualize the sound moving from your first chakra to your third. This helps to associate the distance of where you are. Do not get frustrated if you feel challenged. It is through practice, association and listening that the ear develops. Continue sliding each interval; Sa Ma Sa, Sa Pa Sa, Sa Dha Sa, Sa Ni Sa. It is great to do this in the shower creating additional resonance and reverberation.

The do or Sa is movable, so any scale can be sung with sargam syllables. Practice the scales, using the sargam syllables if you are a musician and want an advanced study. There is a list of exotic scales in the Music Improvisation section. No need to rush; you can get a lot of mileage out of singing the major scale very slowly while deep listening. If you are a beginner, stay with singing the major scale. This can be done for a lifetime with much benefit. You may be surprised how this practice may transport you toward the Divine.

Color is another magical vibrational tool for healing that is powerful in itself or combined with sound. As with sound, there are many different theories on color for healing. The rainbow color system is a practice corresponding the seven colors of the rainbow with the seven chakras, just as we have explored seven notes in the scale.

Chakra balancing with color

Light vibrates faster than sound. Light is the Source of color. Colors are created by how much they absorb or reflect light. Color is a powerful tool for producing healing effects. The colors affect the aura – a subtle energy field that surrounds the body. The chakras regulate the energy coming in and out of the aura.

There are seven rays from the sun, which can be seen through a rainbow. These seven colors correspond to the seven chakras. The colors of the rainbow are ROYGBIV – red, orange, yellow green, blue, indigo and violet. Red has the slowest vibration; as you move up the spine, each color vibrates faster.

1st C	Sa	Root	Red
2nd D	Re	Belly	Orange
3rd E	Ga	Diaphragm	Yellow
4th F	Ma	Chest	Green
5th G	Pa	Throat	Bright Blue
6th A	Dah	Brow	Indigo Blue
7th B	Ni	Crown	Violet

Visualizing colors has a healing effect. Each color has its own frequency and vibration.

Disease disturbs the energy or frequency of the chakra or organ. By applying or visualizing the associated color frequency the body can be stimulated or relaxed back to balance. The colors both effect our organs, nervous system and can influence emotions. Colors assist the body, mind and spirit to heal.

Aura Color Meditation

Take 3 slow deep cleansing breaths. Imagine a waterfall of rainbow colors. Experience each color of the rainbow (red, orange, yellow, green, blue, indigo. violet) one at a time washing away any debris or stuck energy. Notice which colors are soothing and which ones are stimulating. Allow any energy that is not for your highest good to wash away.

Chakra Painting

Tune into each chakra. What does it look like or feel like? What color is it? As you look at each picture write about what you see.

Color Meditation

- *Take 3 slow deep cleansing breaths.*
- *Imagine a red ball of light cleansing and balancing the 1st chakra.*
- *Imagine an orange ball of light cleansing and balancing the 2nd chakra.*
- *Imagine a yellow ball of light cleansing and balancing the 3rd chakra.*
- *Imagine a green ball of light cleansing and balancing the 4th chakra.*
- *Imagine a light blue ball of light cleansing and balancing the 5th chakra.*
- *Imagine an Indigo ball of light cleansing and balancing the 3rd eye.*
- *Imagine a violet ball of light cleansing and balancing your crown.*

How do you feel after imaging the colors? Do you feel relaxed? Do different colors feel differently? Could you see the colors? Did you feel energy moving? Did you sense the colors? Everyone perceives differently. With practice you will increase what you notice. Color is so powerful. It is amazing how changes can be felt by simply imaging colors.

You can bring colors into your aura and chakras through visualization. The aura and chakras can receive color vibrations through thought and intention. This is effective whether you can see the color or not. Some of us visualize more through feeling than seeing. The more you practice color visualization, the more you will notice. Once you can feel the energy readily, begin to combine sound with the colors as in the chart above.

The aura is energy surrounding a person or object. Imagining colors around the body help balance and strengthen this energy as well as clear debris out of the aura.

How do you feel after imaging the colors? Do different colors feel differently? If you are attracted or feel relaxed by a particular color, use this color on a regular basis to clear.

What colors do you have in your house or do you like to wear? These are probably colors you need. Are there any colors that you are not as fond of? Notice if the color you like the least is correlated with the area in the body where you could use some attention. Intentionally bring more of this color into your life. Notice what colors you eat. You many need to intentionally eat more of a certain color to strengthen the body. When walking in nature, imagine nourishing your chakras and aura with the colors around you. One way to bring color into your environment is to get a crystal prism and hang it in the window. It will make the rainbow spectrum on your wall when the sun shines through it. It is magical to see the colors reflected on the wall.

When we are painting and creating visual art with color, we are nourishing the chakra as we are focusing on the colors. Try making a painting using all the colors in the rainbow. Then make a painting with a color you are least drawn to. Notice how you feel.

Stained Glass Mosaics

Stained glass is a wonderful way to bring concentrated colors into your home. Churches have been aware of the sacred qualities in stained glass colors for centuries. The intensity of the colors change throughout the day. You can make yourself a stained glass mosaic to hang in a window.

Hang or place the framed stained glass picture in the window. The colors will change and intensify throughout the day, depending on the sun. It can also be hung on the wall or held in a frame holder. It is more effective if it is back-lit. Stained glass is so beautiful and the colors are so powerful and intense. This is why you see stained glass in churches; the power of the colors assist in creating the sacred.

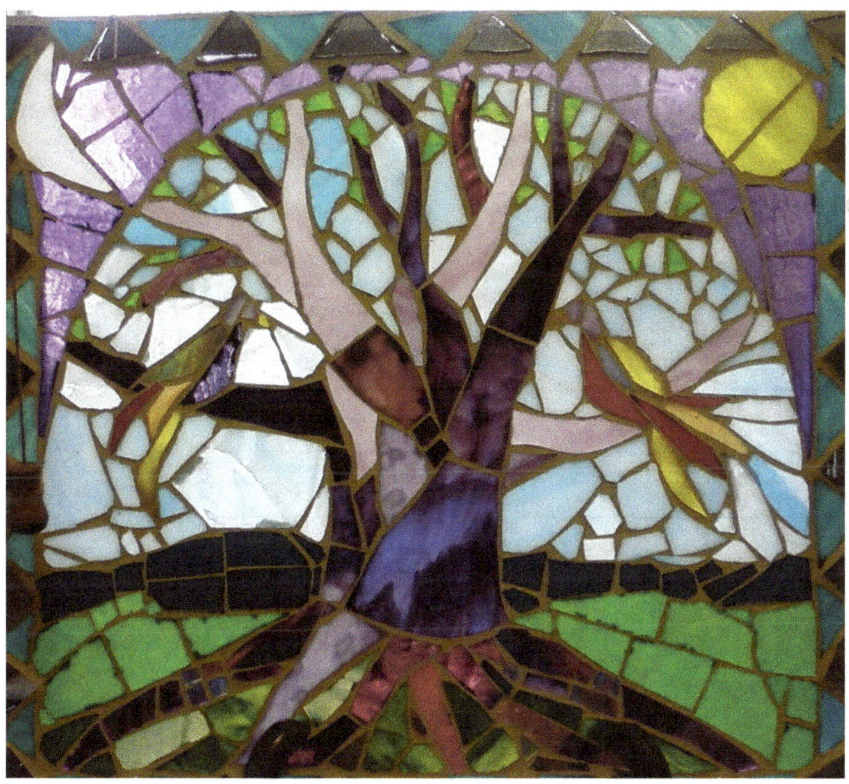

Stained glass, Lynn Miller

Making a Stained Glass Mosaic

Buy a picture frame, and take out the cardboard backing. Wearing goggles, cut thin colored glass sheets with a glass cutter and nippers. (Stained glass comes in separate colored sheets; find a vendor on the internet or local craft store.) Make your design free form or draw a simple outline drawing to put under the glass for your pattern. Glue the colored glass onto the clear glass with transparent glue. (I prefer Uhu glue.) Leave a ¼-inch space between each piece of glass. Once dry, grout it. Spread the grout with a sponge, being sure to fill in all the cracks. Once it is fairly dry, brush away the extra grout with a rag and shine the glass.

I studied vibrational healing with Joy Gardner, author of ***Vibrational Healing through the Chakras.*** In the vibrational healing training we studied the vibrational tools of light, sound, crystals and aromatherapy. This is where I was introduced to chromatherapy. Chromotherapy is a color therapy that applies therapeutic color treatments on the body with colored lights. ***Let There be Light,*** written by Darius Dinshah is an account of the work of his father, Dinshah Ghadiali. A Hindu scientist, Dinshah developed the spectro-chrome system in which one color is tonated for one hour on a particular area of the body through colored filters over a light source. Dinshah, using a combination of 5 colors, formulated 331 color formulas for more than 400 health conditions. Plans on how to make a colored lamp are in the book or it is possible to simply use a colored light bulb. I use color tonation regularly on myself, experiencing dramatic results. At the least, my body completely relaxes after sitting under the colored light. The colors strengthen the colors in the aura.

Crystals and gemstones

Crystals and gemstones have a high vibrational rate that resonate the chakras like sound and color. They can also be combined with sound and intention to increase the energy. Gemstones are colors from the earth. The colors are beautiful and intense. Start a crystal collection of the rainbow colors and learn about their healing properties. The stones are here to help us, as the earth is here to support us. It is amazing how many of the properties can assist on the emotional, physical and spiritual realm through the stone. State an intention for the stones to help clear and balance the chakra. Tell the stones what you would like them to do. Place them on the chakra area that needs balancing. Notice if you feel any sensations or energy moving. Here are a few stones recommended for each chakra. Another way to choose stones are to go to the ones you are drawn to. Hold them and feel their energy. Ask them what they could help you with.

1st	Red or black	smoky quartz, black obsidian, hematite, garnet
2nd	Orange	cat's eye, carnelian
3rd	Yellow	gold calcite, citrine,
4th	Green/pink	rose quartz, jade, rhodochrosite
5th	Blue	lapis lazuli, sodalite, azurite, melachite
6th	Indigo blue	amethyst, moonstone
7th	Violet /white	quartz crystal

A great way to absorb their properties and learn about gemstones is through wearing jewelry. You can make your own. Gemstone beads are so beautiful. Read about the healing properties of the beads. Choose the ones you are energetically drawn to or purposefully pick them through their healing properties. Combine different complimentary colors and healing properties of the beads in your design.

Beading is very meditative. While beading, focus on it's healing properties. Once it is made, you get the reward of wearing it or giving it to a friend.

Have you ever thought about how long a stone has been in the ground? How long it took for it to form before it reached the moment that it is with you. They have infinite wisdom to share with you.

Healing for ourselves and the planet

As each individual does ones own healing, this will assist, collectively, in the healing of our planet. How we feel about ourselves inside is reflected outside in our environment. Self-care = care for the planet. When we sing, the earth is resonating with us. When we dance, we are connecting with the ground. Imagine when we express through color, we are moving pigment which is reflected off light. Light travels close to 700 million miles per hour – a lot of power! Sound travels 768 miles per hour, depending on temperature.

There are miracles everywhere in our everyday life. Expressing ourselves through the arts will bring more harmony on this planet. This practice was done regularly with earth-based cultures in times before us.

Love is a vibrational frequency that connects us with Source energy. Light is a carrier of love. Connect with the light and the energy of the sun and moon.

As the Beatles put it, "All you need is love, love is all you need, love is all you need."

Love is difficult to define in words as with all great things in life. When my parents described Santa Claus, they said he is love. The ability to give and receive is a part of love. Caring for self, others and the environment is part of love. Light is love. Nature is love. The creator is love. We are love as we are a part of the Divine. By chanting "I am love," it gives the experience of love – what it feels like to be love.

I am Love chant

- *Imagine breathing in and out light, adding a shimmer of gold from the sun or silver from the moon.*
- *Imagine this light all around you.*
- *Very slowly chant" I am" on one pitch, continuously.*
- *Add the word love," I am love" as you connect in the heart.*

When I am giving sound healing sessions, I am often guided to sing to the person that they are loved and that they are love. Sometimes I send the message through intention, saying it inwardly. This acknowledgement can create more love for this person if they embrace it. Most of us are confused about love because it came with conditions. Make a practice of loving unconditionally. No judgment, no right or wrong, total acceptance. The exercises in the book are a path to discover this acceptance. Love your art, your music, your dance, yourself and the colors and sounds around you. The arts are an expression of the soul. With acceptance, the soul will come out and dance with you.

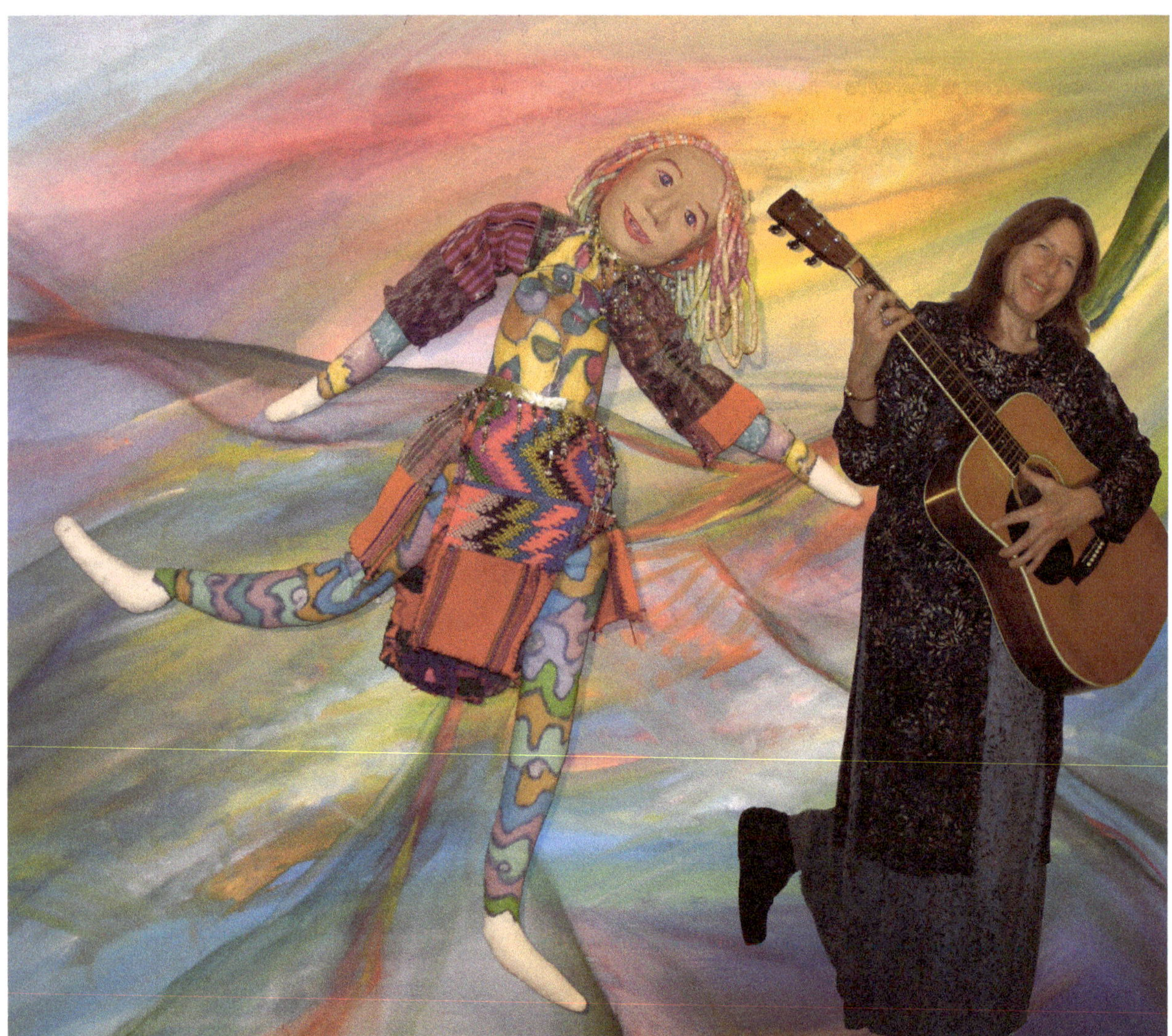

Soul doll in painting, Lynn Miller

SpiritArts and Life Integration

Arts Expression is transformative

The skills and philosophy of ***SpiritArts*** gives lessons on how the Divine works through us. This same philosophy can be applied toward all of life. When we live life in full expression, we are living our life purpose. The arts are a natural form for us to express ourselves. Most of us grew up with expectations and false belief systems by well-meaning families and institutions. Through the arts, we can uncover and rediscover who we really are. Expressing rather than repressing develops a wider range of motion in our lives. This motion gives us life force energy. This life force energy connects us to all things. We all have an innate wisdom and creative intelligence that is available to us for healing. ***SpiritArts*** connects us to this inner essence, our souls, and liberates us to the sacred nature of ourselves.

In the Western culture, we have been taught that only what we can prove or understand is real. What is also real is the magic, the unknown, the imagination. What is real is that we don't understand everything and that we don't always need to know. The need to know distracts us from knowing, from hearing our innate wisdom and trusting the process. Through experiencing our feelings, our stories, our fears and making friends with our imagination, rather than mistrusting it, we express our lives more fully. Soul and spirit do not communicate through linear language. Spirit language is through the imagination world. The more we are open to the realm of unlimited possibilities, the more opportunity there is. It is possible to change the paradigm, to create miracles.

First we have to believe we can. Can you believe that you can play beautiful music without years of musical training? Can you believe you can create a satisfying dance or painting without having years of experience? Can you believe you can assist healing an illness through imagining and feeling yourself healed? All of this is possible when you create through: Breath-Body awareness-Heart Connection-Deep Listening. This is true whether working on healing an illness or creating a piece of art. Be open to the possibility that all things are possible.

Take time to slow down in these accelerated times. Make friends with silence and deeply listen. You will be guided and discover your own inner knowing. It is important to create stillness in order to develop this relationship. Start from silence when beginning to create. The breath helps silence the mind. When we experience something more fulfilling than we originally imagined emerge out of the unknown, we develop trust and spontaneity. The need to control lessens as we learn to trust. Spontaneity is an important life skill. In life, we never really can control anything, even though we may like to. Life will bring challenging experiences. Clinging to the past or what we feel is safe only creates more turbulence. Repeat the mantra, "I am willing to change, I am willing to accept change." After all, this is the only thing we can really count on. It is the ability to bounce back, rebound or let it bounce off that builds strength.

Apply the ***SpiritArts*** approach to your life through:

- **Opening your heart:** Love and accept where you are in your life.
- **Allow**: Make friends with what is going on with self.
- **Surrender:** Realize there is something greater than yourself with which you can co-create. You don't have to do it all. You have help. Just ask.
- **Play:** Do something you enjoy. Have fun. Laugh at yourself once in a while. Laugh in general.
- **Be present**: This will take you out of past or future worries.
- **Tell the truth**: Truth empowers you.
- **Gratitude:** Be grateful for what you do have in your life. When we can approach life without judgment, we find meaningfulness and purpose in even the smallest things on earth.
- **Oneness:** We are all connected. We are not as separate as some may think. Work toward consciousness toward all living things and all beings on this planet. We are all in it together.
- **Trust:** Everything is in perfect order.

The practices in this book are developed to assist one in being present. As Ram Daas put it so well in his book, ***"Be Here Now."*** Our mind loves to hang out in the past or future even though there is nothing but the present moment. The past or the future are only thoughts happening in the present moment. See how the magic begins when we follow our intuition and open to life's possibilities. As our sensory awareness is developed through color, sound and movement, all of our awareness develops which brings expansion. When we raise our vibrations through sound, color and body awareness and release old patterns and belief systems that do not serve us, we raise our consciousness. As our consciousness rises, our frequencies rise, giving us the ability to manifest our dreams. We can change the world one person at a time. As more and more people develop awareness, the collective consciousness changes to create heaven on earth. Amen and Ahwomen.

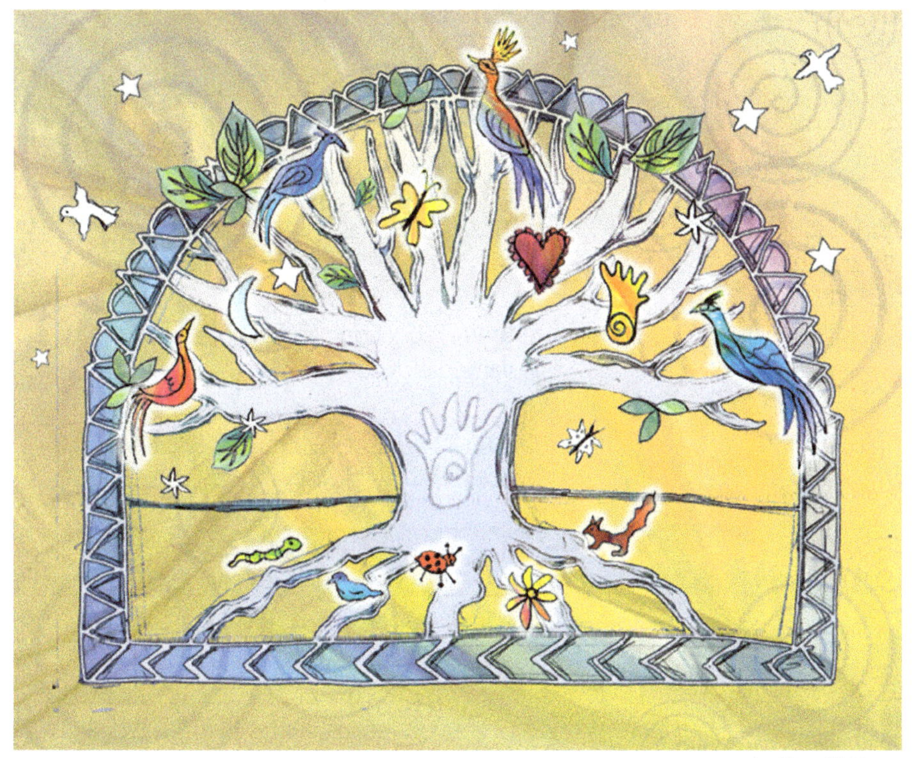

Joy Tree, Jill Carter

References and Suggested Reading

Adler, J. (1999). ***Who is the Witness.*** In (ed), Authentic Movement (pp.141-159). Philadelphia: Jessica Kingsley.

Allen, Pat B. (1995). Art is a Way of Knowing . Boston: Shambala.

Arrian, Angeles (1993) The Four Fold Way: Walking the Path of the Warrior, Teacher, Healer, and Visionary, San Francisco: Harper One Publishers.

Benzwie, Teresa (1987). A Moving Experience, Tucson: Zephr Press.

Campbell, Don (1995). Music: Physician for Times to Come, Wheaton, IL: Quest Books.

Childre, Doc (1998). Freeze-Frame: One Minute Stress Management: A Scientifically Proven Technique for Clear Decision Making and Improved Health.

Chodorow, J. (1999). To Move and Be Moved. In P. Pallaro (ed.), Authentic Movement (pp.267-278). Philadelphia: Jessica Kingsley.

Cutler, Cheryl (2007). Creative Listening: Overcoming Fear in Life & Work, Gainesville, FL: InstaBook Publisher.

Dass, Ram (1971). Be Here Now, San Cristobal, NM: Lama Foundation.

Dinshah, Darius (1996). Let There Be Light, Dinshah Health Society.

Emoto, Masaru (2008). The True Power of Water: Healing and Discovering Ourselves, Parsippany, NJ: Pocket Books.

Frediani, Elizabeth (2008). Where Body Meets Soul, Singing Mountain Publishing Alliance.

Gardner, Joy (1993). The Healing Voice: Traditional and Contemporary Toning, Chanting, and Singing, New York: Random House.

Gardner, Joy (2006). Vibrational Healing Through the Chakras: With Light, Color, Sound, Crystals, and Aromatherapy, New York: Random House.

Gold, Aviva (1998). Painting From the Source, New York: Harper Collins.

Goldman, Jonathan (2002). Healing Sounds: The Power of Harmonics, Rochester, VT: Healing Arts Press.

Hale, Susan (1995). Song and Silence. Albuquerque: La Alameda Press.

Hay, Louise (1984). You Can Heal Your Life. Santa Monica CA: Hay House.

Ingerman, Sandra (2001). Medicine for the Earth: How to Transform Personal and Environmental Toxins, New York: Crown Publishing Group.

Ingerman, Sandra (2010.) Awakening to the Spirit World: The Shamanic Path of Direct Revelation, Boulder, CO: Sounds True Publishing.

Keyes, Elizabeth Laurel (1973). Toning, the Creative Power of the Voice, Camarillo, CA: DeVorss & Company.

Khalighi, Daria Halprin (1989). Coming Alive: The Creative Expression Method, Kentfield, CA: Tamalpa Institute Press.

Knysh, Mary, (2013). Innovative Drum Circles. Bloomsburg, PA: Rhythmic Connections Publishing.

McGinty W. (1998). ***The Body in Analysis: Authentic Movement and Witnessing in Analytic Practice.*** Journal of Analytic Psychology Volume 43, pp. 239-260

McNiff, S. (1981). The Arts and Psychotherapy, Springfield: Charles C. Thomas.

McNiff, Shaun (1992). Art as Medicine, Creating a Therapy of the Imagination. Boston: Shambala.

McNiff, S. (1998). Trust the Process: An Artist's Guide to Letting Go, Boston: Shambhala.

Miller, Eric. (2011). Bioguided Music Therapy. A Practioner's Guide to the Clinical Integration of Music and Biofeedback, London: Jessica Kingsley.

Nachmanovitch, S. (1990). Free Play. The Power of Improvisation in Life and the Arts, Los Angeles: Jeremy Tarcher, Inc.

Oshinsky, Jim (2004). Return to Child: Music for People's Guide to Improvising Music and Authentic Group Leadership. Goshen, CT: Music for People.

Rogers, Natalie (1993). The Creative Connection: Expressive Arts as Healing, Palo Alto, CA: Science and Behavior Books.

Roseman, Ed (2005). Edley's Music Theory for Practical People, Musical EdVentures.

Roth, Gabriel (1997). Sweat your Prayers New York: Tarcher/Putnam.

Sha, Zhi Gang (2007). Soul Wisdom New York: Simon and Shuster.

Whitehouse, Mary (1999). ***Creative Expression in Physical Movement is Language Without Words***. In Pallaro (ed), Authentic Movement (pp. 33-40) Philadelphia: Jessica Kingsley.

Williamson, Marrianne (1992) A Return To Love: Reflections on the Principles of A Course in Miracles, New York: Harper Collins.

It Takes a Village to Write a Book

Speaking of gratitude…..

I have so many people who have supported me through this journey. Fabulous singer, Jan Hittle was instrumental in helping me to organize the text in formatting, editing, and artistic support. Sue Mistretta, Expressive arts therapist provided an insightful peer review. I had editing assistance from Carol Butterworth, my sister-in-law Andrea Price and my dear friend Cheryl Rillo who passed before I finished. My extraordinary mother-in-law Felicia DeMay completed the final formatting. I would also like to thank Mia Bosna for taking many of the photos and photoshopping the doll images into my paintings. They all did this as a labor of love. My amazing artist sister-in-law Jill Carter (Jillcarterdesign.com) designed the book cover and layout. I thank my mother and son for their love and I must thank my husband Eric Miller for continuously asking the question, "did you finish that book yet?" "Yes we did!"

About the Artist

Lynn Miller is a vocalist, guitarist, dancer and visual artist with a passion for improvisation. She is a performer, teacher and healer. She is a music therapist and served as adjunct faculty in the music therapy department at Immaculata University in PA. Lynn is the co-founder of Expressive Therapy Concepts, a non-profit organization with the mission of bringing the healing power of the arts to the community. She is on staff with Music for People, an improvisation certificate training program in the US and in Europe. Lynn also instructs at the FluteHaven Native Flute School and conducts SpiritArts workshops for finding your inner artist and musician.

Go to www.SpiritArts.US for information on workshops, purchase Lynn's CD, ***Mystic Song*** or purchase magical easy to play instruments and hand painted healing drums.

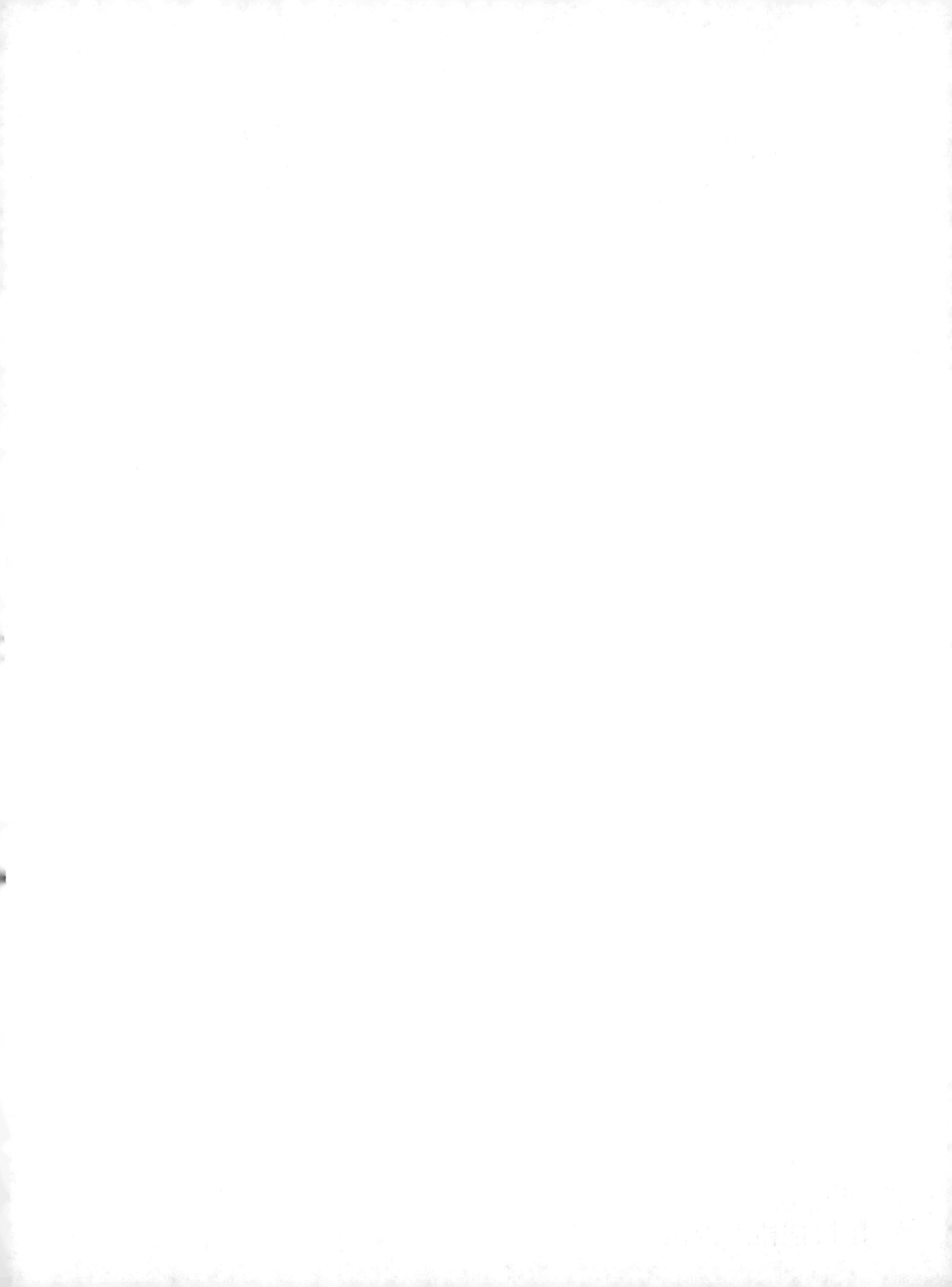

www.ingramcontent.com/pod-product-compliance
Lightning Source LLC
LaVergne TN
LVHW081300100826
845148LV00005B/932